Beatrice Harraden

Things Will Take a Turn

A Story for Children

Beatrice Harraden

Things Will Take a Turn
A Story for Children

ISBN/EAN: 9783337215668

Printed in Europe, USA, Canada, Australia, Japan

Cover: Foto ©Thomas Meinert / pixelio.de

More available books at **www.hansebooks.com**

THINGS WILL TAKE A TURN

A STORY FOR CHILDREN

BY

BEATRICE HARRADEN

AUTHOR OF "SHIPS THAT PASS IN THE NIGHT", "IN VARYING MOODS", ETC.

WITH FORTY-SIX ILLUSTRATIONS
BY J. H. BACON

NEW YORK
CHARLES SCRIBNER'S SONS
1898

MANHATTAN PRESS
474 W. BROADWAY
NEW YORK

PREFACE

TO NEW AND REVISED EDITION.

I have taken the opportunity kindly offered me by the publishers to revise the text of this little story, which was written more than five years ago, and published by them in a series of tales for children.

I had forgotten Childie, and the old bookseller, and the bird-fancier with the red nose, and Mrs. White with the terrifying bonnet, and James the footman with the stiff neck. But now, reading the little book once more, memories of my old friends come back to me; and I fancy I can see Childie,—as I often saw her,—standing at the door of the second-hand book-shop, and looking out anxiously for customers, or waving her handkerchief to Mr. Jones, or smiling at some bit of fun which she and the bird-fancier had in common.

But the little narrow street has been pulled down, and the bird-shop and the book-shop have given place to more stately buildings. So that I and my readers would search in vain for the queer old dwelling where the parrot was taught to say: '*Things will take a turn!*'

BEATRICE HARRADEN.

June 5th, 1894.

CONTENTS.

Chap.		Page
I.	The Old Book-shop,	11
II.	Rosebud's New Friend,	27
III.	Rosebud prepares for High Life,	37
IV.	Mr. Dighton's Housekeeper,	56
V.	Violet and Rosebud,	73
VI.	The Wonderful Parrot,	85
VII.	Mr. Jones visits Grosvenor Square,	95
VIII.	A Chapter of Pleasant Surprises,	113
IX.	A New Lease of Life,	130
X.	A Pleasant Prospect,	142
XI.	Grand-dad's Dream comes True,	148
XII.	The Old and the New,	159

LIST OF ILLUSTRATIONS.

FULL-PAGE ILLUSTRATIONS.

	Page
"Childie waited in breathless anxiety whilst he examined every book,"	29
"Thank you, Rosebud, for making my little girl happy,"	80
"The doctor came to see him and looked grave,"	113
"Ain't I just proud to see you, that's all!"	139

ILLUSTRATIONS IN THE TEXT.

"She spent her time in patching them up,"	11
"Childie had seen him give back the book together with the money,"	14
"Childie put her arms round grand-dad's neck,"	16
"She fetched him his rusty hat and his stick,"	19
"Mr. Jones," she said, "your sleeve is torn,"	21
"The dear little face . . . became once more anxious and sad,"	25
"If you please, sir, I will serve you,"	26
"Meantime do you take this 'ere soup,"	35
"Grand-dad then sneezed several times,"	39
"Good gracious! I've been treading on your doll!"	45
"Do let me give Bully a hemp seed—just one, Mr. Jones,"	50
"He stooped down and kissed her very gently,"	55
"She was lifted on to the sofa by the window,"	57
"This is my friend Mr. Jones,"	63
"Mrs. White smiled and closed her eyes,"	65
"He found her dolls in a corner of the shop,"	68
"If you please, Miss, I've come,"	72
"Here is a doll I want you very much to have,"	77
"Mr. Jones whirled her round and round,"	84

"Things 'ave took a turn,—'urrah! Say that, Donkey,"	90
"He lit his pipe and offered the match to grand-dad,"	91
"He heard some wonderful sounds,"	94
"Mr. Jones went into fits of laughter,"	101
"Nice, tidy, pretty room this is, to be sure!"	107
"Childie was kneeling. . . . kissing his dear hands,"	111
"Sick folks like a whole sight of flowers in their sick-room,"	116
"Mr. Jones, slipping off his boots, crept upstairs,"	118
"Mr. Jones, dear, they say he is very ill,"	119
"Mr. Dighton carried her tenderly downstairs,"	122
"Seizing the biggest book he could find, he placed her feet upon it,"	125
"There, you've been and told, said Mr. Jones, shaking his fist,"	128
"She took them out of a private drawer, and put them tidy,"	135
"Grand-dad came down . . . . leaning on Childie's arm,"	143
"Do you think Rosebud will consent to come, Mrs. White?"	149
"Mr. Dighton found Childie alone, putting the books in order,"	151
"He blew his red nose very violently,"	156
"Her little head was resting against his cheek,"	161

CHAPTER I.

THE OLD BOOK-SHOP.

There was no denying it that trade was bad in the little tumble-down old second-hand book-shop in a poor street of London. Even little Rose Burnley, a ten-year-old lass, with large, wondering eyes, and a smile which was more often sad than merry, knew that things were not going on prosperously in grand-dad's shop. I think she troubled more about them than he did; for he was always reading. I suppose he thought that as he could not sell the books, he might just as well read them and make some use of them. It was a pity they should lie there idle. They were not good-looking books: they were old, and grubby, and worn, and had several names of the past owners written inside, and the second-hand price scratched in pencil on the title-page. Nowadays, when one can buy new copies so cheaply, these fusty, musty old things do not seem very attractive, do they? Ah well, we ought not to abuse them, for they have lived their lives and done their work well.

And little Rose loved them all. She had a profound reverence for the very oldest; and when she was not reading, or seeing after grand-dad, she spent her time in patching them up. She was quite clever at making covers for them, and grand-dad himself said she ought to have been a binder. There was one dilapidated volume—I think it was Clarendon's *History of the Great Rebellion*—which she restored in a marvellous way. Up to now this had been the triumph of her life, although I am not sure whether she was not as well pleased with her success in doctoring a forlorn Greek dictionary, which she respected all the more because she could not understand one single word in it. No, she was not a Greek scholar; but she was an English scholar in her own little way, and she could read aloud as well as any grown-up person, and she was not in the least frightened at long words. She read aloud to her dolls. Good gracious! I really tremble to think what intellectual beings she had made of them. She had rather odd names for them; her two favourites were called Robinson Crusoe and Jane Eyre.

She often envied them.

"You have no worries," she said. "You don't get up every morning, wondering, wondering whether anyone will come and buy some books. And it is all the same to you whether grand-dad looks happy or troubled."

But grand-dad was really unhappy this fine June morning; for money was becoming very scarce, and no one came to the second-hand book-shop. Ah, and there I am wrong.

People certainly did come, only they came to *sell* books, not to *buy* them, and seemed rather

injured when shrivelled-up old David Burnley refused their offers. Why, he had not any money to spare now. He had not enough for Childie and himself. But in the days gone by, when starved-looking students begged him to buy their most precious volumes for a mere song, Childie, as he called his little grand-daughter, had often stood by, and seen him give back the book together with the money. She thought that very sweet of him, and loved him for it.

But, you know, this was not the way to get on in life. His neighbours told him so. They thought him rather a silly old man.

"He has read too much," they said to each other. "Of course he is silly!"

That was their way of looking at the matter; but they were ignorant folk, and knew more about Dutch cheeses and tinned sardines than they did about books! Anyway, to-day he was very troubled about his affairs; he could not fix his attention on his book. He kept looking at Childie, who sat by his side on a footstool, mending Robinson Crusoe's coat. Poor coat! it was even shabbier than grand-dad's coat; and that was saying a good deal. He kept looking at Jane Eyre, who was lying flat on her back, gazing intently at the murky ceiling of the old book-shop. She was very shabby too. They were all shabby and poor, and rather hungry, let me tell you. He combed his thin,

white hair with his thin hand, and then stroked his brow.

"Childie," he said gently, "times are very bad."

In a moment Robinson Crusoe and his coat were thrown on the ground, and Childie sprang up, and put her arms round grand-dad's neck and kissed him.

"I know, dear," she whispered.

"It was easy enough to get along while there was money in the till," he said, smiling at her sadly, "and one did not trouble much then. But the quarter's rent is due soon, and there is very little to pay it with, Childie. I have been thoughtless and selfish. There is nothing easier in the whole world than to be selfish. Kiss me again, Childie, and tell me that you do not love me any the less because I have been selfish."

"Why, grand-dad," she said, as she kissed him lovingly, "it has not been your fault if people have not come to buy our books. And every one says trade is bad, you know. I went in to look at the birds in Mr. Jones's shop, and he told me he had not sold a single one during the last few days. I felt sorry for him, for he is very kind although he has got a red nose. And what a red nose it is, to be sure, grand-dad! But *he* was not in the dumps. He said to me: 'Look you, Rosebud child, things will take a turn.' He is always saying this to me; and, fancy, grand-dad, he has taught that parrot of his to say: 'Things will take a turn'. We must say it and believe it too. Do you hear, grand-dad?"

"Yes, Childie," he answered, smiling. "Now I am going out to try and get together some money which has been owing me a long time. It is not much, but it is better than nothing. You mind the shop—you and Jane Eyre and Robinson Crusoe. There will not be a great deal for you to do," he added with a sigh; "no one is likely to come."

Quick as thought she fetched him his rusty hat, and his stick, and his horrid little snuff-box; and off he started on his journey.

"Oh," she said to herself, as she stood at the shop door, watching that dear, bent figure trudging wearily along, "if I could only sell a book whilst he is away, how glad and proud I should be!"

And the tears darted to her eyes; but she

brushed them hastily from her face, for she heard the parrot over the way screeching: "Things will take a turn! Things will take a turn!" And

Mr. Jones, the happy possessor of the red nose and the bird-shop, seeing his little friend standing at the door, crossed over the road to speak with her.

"Good-morning, Rosebud," he said gently. "How's yourself?"

"Quite well, thank you, Mr. Jones," she answered smiling. "And you?"

"Fust-rate," he answered. "Last night I sold a pair of Norwich canaries and a bishop—you know that fat, sleek fellow with a yellow crest. And I tell you, Rosebud child, them bishop birds bring in a sight of money, they do. I should like to sell a dozen or two every jolly morning. But upon my soul, littl'un, prosperity is peeping round the corner. Time it should too. And how's the grand-dad?"

"Oh, pretty well," she said. "He has gone out and left me in charge."

"And ain't you just proud?" he said, looking kindly at her. "Fancy you being left in charge—a bit of a bird like you! Why, if I had you in a cage with some fine feathers on, I'd make a bet you'd fetch more than a Norwich canary, or a weaver, or a bishop, or a pope, or a piping bull-finch, or a Virginian nightingale, or all of them put together."

"Mr. Jones," she said, "your sleeve is torn. Perhaps you had better wait while I mend it."

"Thank you, hearty," he said, as he sank into

grand-dad's chair at the back of the tiny counter; "this ain't the first piece of stitching you've done for me, is it? You're fond of your needle, ain't you? And you're fond of me too, in a sort of a way?"

"Of course I am fond of you," she said laughing. "We are fond of all those who are kind to us."

"Are we now?" remarked Mr. Jones. "Well, I suppose you ought to know, as you have read a whole sight of books; but all *I* know is that many folk has been kind to me in my life, and I'm blest if I've been fond of them, or grateful to them for the matter of that!"

"What a horrible person you must really be!" said Rosebud, putting down his coat and looking up at him.

"That may be," he laughed, "but I ain't no exception. Why, your little fingers have been quick! Thank you kindly. I say, Rosebud child, do the dolls like chocolate or toffee best?"

"They have not a sweet tooth," she said as she helped him on with his coat, and watched him gazing admiringly at her work. "In fact, Mr. Jones, if you look at Jane Eyre and Robinson Crusoe, you'll find they have not any teeth at all."

"Then I'm blessed if soup ain't the best thing for them to have!" he answered. "But what can you expect at their time of life? They look as if they'd come out of the ark, they do."

"They are not as young as they might be, Mr. Jones," she laughed; "but they are none the worse for that."

"That's right, missy," he replied; "always speak up for your friends."

And having wished her good luck for the morning, and bestowed a patronizing pat on the heads of Jane Eyre and Mr. Crusoe, who were looking rather sulky at his rude remarks about them, Mr. Jones took his departure to his place of business over the other side of the road. And Childie set to work to dust the second-hand books.

She tried to be kind and just to them all, but it was very hard to take any interest in those disagreeable, dull school-books. She could not get up any enthusiasm for *Cornwell's Geography* and *Mangnall's Questions* and Mrs. Markham's *History of England*, but she did her duty by them.

And all the time she was thinking how proud she should be if only she had some money to show grand-dad on his return. And the dear little, fair face, which had brightened up at Mr. Jones's visit, became once more sad and anxious—very anxious.

"Are all people anxious?" she thought to herself, as she sat down on her stool, and rested her elbows on her knees, and stared at the bookshelves. "I wonder whether the people who write books are as worried as the people who try to sell them and can't. Oh, if I were only grown-up, and could work for grand-dad! He should read all day, and never have any worries. And I'd buy him a new snuff-box and a new velvet skull-cap to keep the cold off his dear head. And he'd look so nice in it too, for grand-dad is handsome; I think he is quite a picture. But he is old now, and he has no one to love him but me, and I am not really old enough to take care of him properly. If one could only become old in a day, or a week, or even a year! It seems to take *such* a long time."

Then she closed her eyes and smiled happily; for it was pleasant to make plans, and her little head was full of schemes and ideas—all for grand-

dad, not for herself, not even for Jane Eyre and Robinson Crusoe.

Suddenly she heard a footstep, and looking up saw a very tall gentleman standing just inside the door. The colour flushed to her cheeks, and her heart beat excitedly, for here, in very truth, was a real customer.

"Is there anyone to serve me?" he said kindly, bending down to her. He had such a way to bend!

"If you please, sir," she said timidly, "I will serve you."

CHAPTER II.

ROSEBUD'S NEW FRIEND.

"You will serve me?" said the tall gentleman, smiling somewhat incredulously. "Well, little girl, I must tell you that I have been looking everywhere for a particular volume to complete a certain edition of Cæsar's works. I suppose you do not happen to know who Cæsar was?"

"Oh, yes," she answered, "of course I do. He crossed the Rubicon. Grand-dad taught me all about him; and then I've read, you know. Here's where we keep his works."

And she pointed to the topmost shelf.

"I'm sorry I can't reach," she said, looking at him mournfully. "It seems very rude of me to ask you to look yourself. But if I had the ladder I would get up at once. Only I cannot carry the ladder myself. Grand-dad generally carries it, and then I hold it while he mounts it. But he is old now, and I am always fearful lest he should tumble."

The tall gentleman—whose name, by the way, was Mr. Dighton—stared in amused astonishment at this quaint little shopkeeper. He was quite pleased with her manner and her appearance.

"And so you know who Cæsar is?" he said. "Well, that is more than my little girl knows. Poor little girl! And she is just about your age, too; only she cannot run about, and mount ladders as you do. She lies on a sofa all through the long day, which is very long for her sometimes."

"I'm sorry," said Childie softly; and the tears came into her eyes. She had such a sympathetic heart.

"Then you must be sad, sir," she said.

"Yes," he answered; "I am very often sad." And he sighed. "Well now, for the book," he added. "We can very well do without the ladder, for I can reach the top shelf with the aid of that footstool."

"CHILDIE WAITED IN BREATHLESS ANXIETY WHILST HE EXAMINED EVERY BOOK."

Childie waited in breathless anxiety whilst he examined every book on the shelf. Oh, how she hoped it would be there!

"It isn't here," he said. "I am disappointed."

And he took his handkerchief from his pocket and rubbed the dust off his hands. He looked rather cross too. I suppose he did not like dust; some people don't.

Childie's face fell. She was also disappointed.

"If you please, sir," she said pleadingly, "it may be on this shelf, or amongst that heap of books. Will you take grand-dad's seat, sir, whilst I look?"

But the book was nowhere to be found. They both searched for it diligently; and it was really quite funny to see Mr. Dighton kneeling on the ground and diving amongst the miscellaneous volumes.

"It is of no use," he said, standing up again. "I might have known that I should not find it here."

Childie's courage had gradually been failing her, and now, overcome with excitement, anxiety, and disappointment, she burst into tears, and cried as though her heart would break.

"Please, sir," she sobbed, "forgive me; but I did so hope to sell a book as a surprise for grand-dad. No one buys books from us now. And trade is very bad, and things don't seem to take a turn, although the parrot over the way says they will. And when you came in I was so proud and glad, because grand-dad has left me in charge; and you are the first customer we've had for a very long time. And now you can't find what you want."

She looked such a poor, sad little lass, that all his kindly pity rose up in his heart.

He took her hand and put it into his own great, big hands, and told her not to cry her blue eyes away, for he wanted another book, which would do just as well; and he pounced upon the first he came to—it happened to be *Mangnall's Questions*, price ninepence—and he put a bright, shining sovereign on the counter, and told her to keep it all for herself and grand-dad.

She smiled through her tears.

"How good you are!" she said, looking up at him. "Only I don't think I ought to take it from you. *Mangnall's Questions* is only ninepence."

"I am quite sure you ought to take it from me," he said kindly as he put the shabby little book into his pocket; for he did not wish to hurt her feelings by not taking it away. "Do you know, I should be ever so angry if you did not keep that gold piece. Why, look at it. It is a jubilee sovereign, quite new and spruce, and will bring you good luck. Yes, I am quite sure it will bring you good luck. Now, tell me your name, little girl?"

"If you please, sir," she said, "my name is Rose; but grand-dad calls me Childie, and Mr. Jones calls me Rosebud."

"Mr. Jones has very good taste," said Mr. Dighton. "And who may he be?"

"If you please, sir," she answered, "Mr. Jones is the bird-fancier over the way. Oh! he has such beautiful birds; only trade is bad with him too. But he has harder times than we have; for birds want feeding, don't they? and books only want dusting. There is Mr. Jones at his shop window. Won't he just be glad to see that I have got a real customer!"

"A real customer!" laughed Mr. Dighton. "Not wax-work, like your poor old dolls. What learned-looking dolls they are too! Do they know about Cæsar crossing the Rubicon?"

Childie laughed merrily.

"Perhaps they do," she said; "only they never tell me what they know. But I've read such a lot to them that I think they can't be altogether stupid!"

"Well, little Rosebud," said the tall gentleman, stooping down and holding out his hand to her, "I must be going home now to my little girl. I shall tell her about you. Perhaps you would like to come and read to her, and help her to spend part of the long day. Somehow or other I don't think she would find it at all sad and wearisome when you were with her. You would be kind to her, wouldn't you, and patient and gentle?"

"Indeed, sir," said Childie earnestly, "I would try to be so."

"Then tell grand-dad," he said, "that I shall come in to-morrow, and speak with him myself. Good-bye, Rosebud. Mind now, there must not be any more tears in those blue eyes."

And he put up his finger as though in solemn warning, and left Childie staring after him in bewilderment.

"How kind he is!" she thought. "It is a long way to look up to his face; but when you once get there, what a kind, good face it is! And how sad he looked when he spoke of his little girl. I shall never forget him."

And she sat down on her stool, and began to put a brown-paper cover on a miserable, tattered book. But the work did not get on very quickly, for I fancy Rosebud was thinking that if people did not have one kind of anxiety, they had another.

"Perhaps the tall gentleman does not have to trouble about customers," she thought; "but then he must always be sad about his little girl."

Then she looked at the bright sovereign, and remembered how pleased and surprised grand-dad would be when he came home and heard all the wonderful news she had to tell him; and her little face shone with June sunshine.

And she sang a snatch of melody, something about the trees and the birds and the flowers. One always sings of them when one is happy.

Suddenly a voice, not so melodious as hers, called out:

"Bless me, Rosebud child! if that ain't a more lovely noise than any my birds could make! Why weren't you a Norwich canary or a Virginian nightingale? You'd just make my fortune—at a handy time, too!"

"Oh, Mr. Jones! you did startle me," she said laughing. "I've such a lot to tell you. The parrot is quite right, for things will take a turn, I am sure."

"Of course they will, Birdie," he said cheerily. "And meantime do you take this 'ere soup, or else I shall drop it. It's for them toothless dolls of yours; but, supposing they ain't got no appetites,

then I guess you and your grand-dad had best make away with it. And as soup ain't good without fresh rolls, so please you, littl'un, I've brought some fresh rolls. Trade is reviving, Rosebud, and so is soup and rolls."

"You are very good," she said gratefully. "Jane Eyre and Robinson Crusoe can't thank you, but I thank you, Mr. Jones. You are always being kind to me."

"Tut, tut!" he answered. "You must run over and tell me about the tall customer. "Oh, there's someone going into my shop! "I'm off, littl'un."

"That soup and them rolls will do her good," he said to himself as he went back to his shop. "She don't look particular strong, dear little lassie; and I'm thinking people don't grow up hearty in fusty old book-shops. Never a day goes by that the sight of that littl'un don't do me good. Bless her heart!"

CHAPTER III.

ROSEBUD PREPARES FOR HIGH LIFE.

Grand-dad had not been successful in getting any money together. Some people, you know, do not trouble in the very least about paying their debts; and it is a cruel and hard thing when the poor have to wait a weary long time before they can get paid for their work. Poor dress-makers complain bitterly about the grand ladies who give them their satins and silks to make, and expect the dresses to be ready in less than no time; but they are quite surprised if they are expected to pay in less than no time. And they often let whole weeks pass by without giving a thought to the little scrawly bill waiting so patiently to be noticed. And it would be nothing to them to take out their purses and pay at once. Nothing prevents them except thoughtlessness and selfishness.

However this may all be, grand-dad came home tired and disappointed. He was chiefly anxious about the child, for he really did not care about himself.

"What is to become of her," he thought, "when the money has all been spent, and there is nothing more coming in?"

No wonder that grand-dad's heart was heavy, and his footstep weary.

There was no one in the shop. He sank down into his chair behind the counter, and took from his pocket his red cotton handkerchief, which he passed over his burning forehead. Then he pulled out his horrid little snuff-box, and refreshed himself with a pinch of snuff. Childie did not like snuff, and always congratulated Robinson Crusoe on the fact that he did not care about it.

"I shall be quite content, Crusoe," she used to say to him in private, "if you take grand-dad as your model in everything except his love for snuff. Do you hear?"

I don't know whether he heard, but he certainly heeded, for he was a total abstainer from snuff!

Grand-dad then sneezed several times, and then

took off his goggle-eyed spectacles and rubbed them with the corner of his red cotton handkerchief. Having made them clean and clear he put them on again, about half-way down his nose. It was always a puzzle to Childie why he should look *over* his spectacles and not *through* them. Sometimes, though, he did not wear them at all, but closed his right eye with the second finger of his right hand and read with his left eye. This puzzled Childie too; she thought it rather hard on that left eye.

"Use both your eyes when *you* read, Robinson Crusoe," she said to him. "I prefer it."

Childie was strict in her own little quiet way. She would have made an excellent schoolmistress.

But to-day grand-dad did not read. He looked mournfully at the second-hand books, and for the first time in his life wished they were all brand-new, uncut, and sprucely dressed, because then he would have a chance of selling them. He had rather despised new books; but this morning he had been gazing into a grand shop of every kind of book—large, small, and medium, good, bad, and indifferent, but fresh and new and beautiful; and he saw so many people going in and coming out again with parcels in their hands, that he quite longed to be the lucky possessor of that shop: just for Childie's sake, not for his own.

"Just for Childie's sake!" he murmured to himself as he took off his boots and thrust his tired old feet into his slippers.

And at that moment she came into the shop.

"What luck, grand-dad?" she said cheerily.

"None for us, child," he answered sadly.

"Ah, you mustn't say that, dear!" she said, picking up the red cotton handkerchief which had fallen to the ground, and putting it into his pocket, as though she were his little mother. "You mustn't say that, for I've had a real customer, and I've a real sovereign to give you; and here it is, grand-dad. So don't ever tell me that I can't keep shop well!"

"What book have you sold, child?" he asked, looking at her wonderingly.

"*Mangnall's Questions*," she answered laughing. "What do you think of that?"

And then she told him the whole story of the tall gentleman's visit, and she begged that he would allow her to go and read to the little invalid girl.

"Of course you shall go, Childie," he said lovingly. "And well might that gentleman wish to have you to read to his little daughter. Where could one hope to find a dearer, sweeter little girl-flower than my Rosebud?"

And off they went, hand in hand, to the backroom to enjoy Mr. Jones's soup and fresh rolls, which Jane Eyre and Robinson Crusoe had declined with thanks.

About twelve o'clock the following morning the tall gentleman called in to see old David Burnley. Childie was not there at the time.

"Your grand-daughter pleased me mightily yesterday," he said kindly, "and I have taken quite a fancy to her. She speaks beautifully. You have indeed taught her well. Now, I should like her to come and see my little girl, who I am sure will be kind to her. My little girl, you know, is an invalid: a motherless invalid. And she cannot read a great deal; for her eyes are weak. And she does not care about all children, but I think she would be fond of your little Rosebud. And Rosebud could read to her, and be her companion for part of the day. I am sure your little granddaughter would be proud to earn some money. And you would let her come, wouldn't you?"

"You are very good, sir," said the old man gently. "Of course I would let her come."

"Just for part of the day," continued Mr. Dighton. "Ah, here is the little woman," he added, as Childie came into the shop. "You see, I have not forgotten you, have I?"

And grand-dad was quite touched to see how kindly he greeted Childie, stooping down and taking her hand and speaking to her so freely and gently. As for Rosebud herself, it seemed to her the most natural thing in the world to see her tall friend again and hear his kind fresh voice; and she chattered away to him as if she had known him all her life.

"I have just been to look at Mr. Jones's new bullfinch," she confided to him. "I wonder what you'd think of it. Now, *I* think it's a beauty, and it pipes such pretty tunes."

"Indeed," he said, smiling at her. "And do you know as much about birds as you do about books?"

She laughed.

"Oh," she answered, "I only know what Mr. Jones tells me. And then one can't help learning a little when one sees all the birds, can one? But sometimes I think it is very cruel to keep them shut up in those tiny cages. But, do you know, Mr. Jones has often put them in bigger cages just to please me. Isn't that nice of him? He laughs at me when I ask him; but he never refuses me. Oh, I remember he was a little cross once. But then he had the toothache dreadfully; and one can't feel very kind when one has the toothache, can one?"

"Certainly not," he replied. "Well, you must take me to see your friend Mr. Jones one day, when he has not got the toothache. I should not like him to be cross with me."

"As if anyone could be cross with you, sir!" she said eagerly. "I am sure I couldn't if I tried all the day long."

"That's all right," he said laughing. "I hope you will always say that. Good gracious! I've been treading on your doll, and I've broken its right arm! What will you say to me now?"

He stooped down and picked up poor Robinson Crusoe, who probably would have groaned if he could; for it is not a particularly pleasant thing to have a crushed arm!

Childie was certainly rather heartless this morning, for she giggled and seemed immensely amused; and even grand-dad laughed to see the tall gentleman holding the wounded doll in his hand, and looking the picture of penitence and misery.

"What will you say to me now?" he asked again. "Won't you feel angry with me now?"

"No," she laughed; "it is all Crusoe's fault for sprawling about on the ground. And it doesn't matter much whether he has one or two arms; he never does any work, you know."

She took the doll from Mr. Dighton and put it safely on the counter; but although she laughed and smiled, I think in her heart of hearts she was really sorry. But she was not going to let him see that; for he had been kind to her, and she was grateful to him.

He stopped a few minutes longer arranging with grand-dad that she should come to his house on the morrow and see his little girl, and then he asked about trade, and seemed sorry to hear that things were so bad.

"But you must cheer up," he said kindly. "By the way, about that book. Suppose you try and get it for me. And I daresay I shall be asking you to look out for several other books for me. I cannot spare the time just at present, and shall be glad of your help. And I'll pay you generously; be sure of that."

Grand-dad's face brightened up with hope and happiness.

"Thank you, sir," he murmured. "Do you know you have come to us just when we wanted help. You have given me back strength and hope. God bless you."

Then Mr. Dighton turned to Childie, pointed to Robinson Crusoe mournfully, and said:

"And you really forgive me, little one, for having squashed that poor doll's right arm?"

"Yes, indeed!" she answered eagerly.

"Ah," he said, as he was leaving the shop, "I expect my little girl will scold me when she hears what mischief I have been doing."

"Don't tell her," said Childie; "and I won't tell her either. Let it be a secret between ourselves."

But he shook his head.

"It's of no use," he replied solemnly. "My little girl guesses all my secrets. Good-bye, Rosebud. My housekeeper shall come and fetch you to-morrow." And he hailed a hansom cab and drove to his beautiful house in Grosvenor Square, all the time thinking to himself what a lucky chance it was that took him to the second-hand book-shop.

"That child will please my little Violet," he said to himself. "She is quaint and gentle; and if ever there was a little lady, she is one. Her clothes are poor and shabby, but they are quite neat. And that white apron she wears is spotless. And what a little mother she seems to be to that scholarly, worn-out old grandfather of hers. How pleased she was to see him smile and look happy when I spoke to him of work. Fancy me now hunting about for a wretched old second-hand book and finding instead a dear little Rosebud. Who would have thought it?"

Childie meanwhile put her stool near grand-dad's arm-chair behind the counter, pulled out her sewing, and began to work diligently.

"Only think, grand-dad," she said, "I shall be able to earn a little money for you before I am grown-up! I always thought people had to wait until they were grown-up before they could be of any use to those they loved."

"Why, Childie," he said lovingly, as he lit his pipe (for she had been out to get him a little tobacco for a treat); "why, Childie, you have been of use to me ever since you were born. You have loved me."

"Is that being useful?" she asked, opening her blue eyes wide.

"Of course it is," answered her grandfather. "It is everything."

In the course of the afternoon Childie ran over

to Mr. Jones's, just to tell him about the tall gentleman's visit, and to have another look at the piping bullfinch.

"And so you're going to that grand gentleman's house?" said Mr. Jones, who was mixing seed for the birds. "I don't suppose you'll want to come and see the old bird-fancier when you've got them new swell friends of yours?"

"What a horrid thing to say, Mr. Jones!" answered Childie reproachfully; but seeing that there was a smile on his face, she added:

"There, I knew you did not mean it! What a tease you are, Mr. Jones! Do you know, my tall gentleman is coming to see you one day when you are not feeling cross. You will let him look at your birds, won't you, Mr. Jones, as he is my friend?"

"Delighted!" replied the gentleman of the red nose. "Any time he likes to come I shall be ready to say a civil word to him. So now you know. And what I say I mean. Don't I, littl'un?"

"Yes, Mr. Jones," she answered. "But you're spilling a lot of that seed. Mayn't I help you? And oh, do let me give Bully a hemp seed—just one, Mr. Jones!"

"You'll spoil that 'ere bird," said Mr. Jones, putting a few hemp seeds into Childie's little hand. "Too many hemp seeds is as bad for them birds as too much beer or sweet stuff is bad for you and me."

"Look here, Rosebud," he said when she had finished feeding the bullfinch, "what I say I mean, don't I? And this is what I say: You always look a little dear; but I want you to look quite spruce to-morrow, for my own honour, you know, and for grand-dad's too. I've found a few shillings tucked away in a seed-tin. Bless me, I was just surprised to find them yesterday! And I said to myself I'm smashed if these sha'n't go to buy something fine for my little Rosebud. Grand-dad don't think of these things; he don't notice. But I notice, bless your heart! I look to the fashings. And I've seen a sweet tidy cape as you must have. Tut, tut, not a word! I'll get old John next door to mind the shop for a half hour; and you and I, we'll just go and buy that sweet pretty thing. Grosvenor Square, indeed!—that's where you're

Rosebud Prepares for High Life. 53

going to! We'll teach Grosvenor Square how to look! And what do you say to a wee rosebud in your hat, littl'un, just to make it spruce and gay?"

Childie clapped her hands with delight; for, like all of us, she was fond of a little bit of finery.

"Only, Mr. Jones," she said, "you ought to spend this money on yourself, for you sadly want a new hat."

"A new hat!" he said, laughing. "Why, Rosebud, what are you thinking about? That hat of mine hanging on that peg ain't more than four year old come September. When it's ten year old, then I shall think it wants cleaning up or seeing to a bit. Come along. How that parrot *do* screech to-day! Folks say the book-business makes one's eyes bad; but deary me, the bird-business does try one's ears!"

They called next door, and asked old John to look after the shop for a short time; and then Mr. Jones, taking Childie's hand, plunged into the linen-draper's a few yards down the street.

"That's the article," he said, pointing to a little black cape. "What do you think of that, Childie?"

"Oh, it's beautiful, Mr. Jones," she said admiringly. "Only it is much too good for me."

"Tut, tut!" he replied.

And he bought it then and there, and made her put it on at once that he might see how she looked in it.

"Fust-rate!" he said, smiling proudly.

And then they bought a little pink rosebud and a pair of gray cotton gloves, and, armed with these wonderful purchases, went back to the bird-shop.

"Don't you say anything to grand-dad," he said as he stooped down and kissed her very gently; "but just you put them fineries on to-morrow and see if he notices. Maybe he won't notice. But there, there! his eyesight is awful bad, you know. And we can't all notice the same things, can we? Why, you know I don't ever take any heed of them seedy-looking books of yours."

Childie thanked him many times for his beauti-

Rosebud Prepares for High Life. 55

ful presents, and went home to grand-dad to get his tea ready. She found him in excellent spirits; for he had three customers, one after the other.

"It certainly does look as if things were taking a turn, Childie," he said, smiling brightly at her. "And it is all through Childie. I am sure of that."

CHAPTER IV.

MR. DIGHTON'S HOUSEKEEPER.

Little Violet Dighton lay on the sofa in her beautiful sitting-room, waiting for her father's return home from his visit to the second-hand bookseller's shop. She was fair-haired and fair-complexioned; her face was thin and pain-weary, and she was slight of form and figure. She wore a pretty blue-coloured silk frock, with a yellow sash round it, and some soft lace at the neck. Her hands were very thin. She had a little gold ring with a pearl in it on the third finger of her right hand. She had been doing some fancy crotchet-work; but I suppose she was tired, for she had let it fall to the ground, and a handsome Persian cat was making sport with the ball. Perhaps that cat knew that Violet could not jump up and run after him!

No, she could not jump up. In the morning she was lifted very gently on to the sofa by the window, and there she stayed all the day long. She was an odd little lady; she could have had

many companions, for people wished to be kind, but she did not care about them all. She liked best to have her father with her, and was quite happy for the whole day if he had found time to spend an hour with her. The whole house was beautiful, but her room was full of wonderful treasures. The walls were hung with pictures; and there were all kinds of books and engravings on the table near her, and lovely vases with fresh flowers in them, and plants here and there and everywhere. At least she had much to look at as she lay on her sofa, and Mr. Dighton seldom came home without bringing her something to please her: a sweet flower, or perhaps a little scented bag, or a new puzzle; she was fond of puzzles and nearly always made them out; and sometimes a new picture would be brought in mysteriously, and he would pretend to know nothing at all about it, when, to tell you the truth, he had spent ever so long in choosing it.

He would have wished above all things to give her health, but he could not do that. It was sad to think that she had everything she could possibly wish for except health.

She was very anxious to see the little girl of whom her father had spoken so much. She was quite fearful lest the old grandfather should not allow Rosebud to come and see her; and so you can imagine how pleased she was when her father came home and told her that he had arranged for Mrs. White, the housekeeper, to go and fetch Rosebud at ten o'clock on the morrow.

"You always say that you are best pleased when I bring you flowers, Violet," said Mr. Dighton as he put a beautiful orchid into a little vase on the table by the sofa; "and I am sure you will like to have the little Rosebud: a little human flower.

"Now, what do you think I have been doing this morning?—I have broken that child's doll. So I went into a doll-shop, and I've bought this concern. And you must give it to her to-morrow. Is it a nice one, Violet?"

"A beauty!" she answered, looking at it admiringly. "How pleased Rosebud will be! Only it has not got a very nice hat on. I think I must make it a new one."

She set to work diligently, and turned out a wonderful thing for the doll's head; and when

Mrs. White, the housekeeper, saw it, she declared solemnly that a court milliner could not have done it better.

Mrs. White started about half-past nine the next morning to go to old David Burnley's shop. Between you and me, she did not quite like the notion of "this chit of a child" coming to the house.

"Master has such odd ideas," she said to herself as she rolled along, for she was rather a stout personage. "Miss Violet is going on very nicely by herself, and doesn't want any strange body coming to worry her. Deary me! what a narrow street to live in!"

I should tell you that years ago Mrs. White had lived in a far narrower street than Childie's; but it was so long ago that she had quite forgotten. People do forget, you know!

She had quite determined to be very stern and patronizing and haughty to the "chit"; and she was almost glad she had a cough, because a certain kind of cough is very awe-inspiring; and she wished to impress Rosebud with a proper sense of her importance. She was dressed in black, and wore a wonderful black bonnet, with a terrifying violet tuft on the top. Her face was broad and flabby, but not unkind-looking, and she had a soft old heart beneath her heavy mantle.

She stopped before the second-hand book-shop and looked in. There was no one there except a little girl, dressed in a gray frock, a black hat, with a tiny pink rosebud in it, and a neat little cross-over cape.

It was rather a warm morning, and Mrs. White was somewhat out of breath. Childie saw this, and fetched a chair, into which the old lady sank with evident satisfaction.

"Thank you, deary," she said between her pants, forgetting all about her resolution to be stern and haughty and patronizing. In fact, one can't be very haughty when one is out of breath, can one?

"I suppose, now, you are little Rose Burnley, whom I've come to fetch?" she asked.

"Yes, if you please," said Childie.

"Well, you've made yourself very neat and tidy," said Mrs. White, looking at her with approval.

"She's always neat and tidy," said a harsh voice.

Mrs. White turned her face to the shop door and saw a red-nosed individual standing on the step.

"Is this your grandfather?" she asked rather stiffly.

"No," answered Childie, going up to the red-nosed individual and putting her hand in his. "This is my friend, Mr. Jones."

"Pleased to make your acquaintance, ma'am." said Mr. Jones, bowing most courteously, and removing his shabby hat from his bald head. "So you are going to march our little Rosebud off with you. Ah! well, ma'am, I'm sure you'll take care of her. Good-bye, Rosebud child. I just popped in to see how them 'ere fineries sat on you, and my word, they do look nice! I'm just as proud as I am when any of my bonny birds have got their new feathers on. Bless me, what a little spruce thing it is, to be sure!"

And he went away grinning with pleasure.

Then Childie came nearer to Mrs. White and said earnestly:

"He is so kind to me, dear good Mr. Jones. Don't you think, ma'am, that there are a great many kind and good people in the world?"

"Perhaps there are," replied Mrs. White, leaving off fanning herself with her handkerchief, and staring curiously at the odd little girl, whose manner was full of trust and confidence.

"Do you know," continued Childie, "Mr. Jones is only cross when he has toothache. Do you ever have toothache, ma'am? I know a wonderful cure which Mr. Jones uses."

"No, child, I'm not troubled with it," said Mrs. White, who had a complete set of false teeth. (But that's a secret between you and me!)

"I'm glad of that," answered Childie smiling; "for it is dreadful to think of people suffering pain. Please, ma'am, does the little lady suffer much pain?"

"Sometimes," said Mrs. White gently. "Come, we must go to her. I am rested now."

"You still look very hot and tired," said Childie in her own little motherly way. "Supposing I fan you?"

And taking a newspaper from the counter, Childie steadily waved it to and fro, and hot Mrs. White smiled and closed her eyes, enjoying the

cool breeze, and pleased with Rosebud's thoughtfulness.

"Why, I declare you're quite a little mother," she said kindly, drawing the child near to her and kissing her. "We must be great friends, mustn't we?"

"If you please, ma'am," answered Childie, "I should like to be friends with you."

"And so you shall," replied Mrs. White, rising from her chair and surveying the books.

"If you are really going, ma'am," said Childie, "I must just call grand-dad to mind the shop. And I am sure he would wish to say good-bye to us."

Mrs. White nodded pleasantly to her, and Rosebud ran into the back-room, and returned in a few minutes followed by grand-dad, who seemed rather nervous at the prospect of addressing a strange lady. He kept quite close to Childie, as though claiming her protection and care. She looked at him affectionately and proudly, keeping her hand in his, and watching anxiously to see whether Mrs. White was impressed by his dear presence.

"This is grand-dad," she said, smiling triumphantly.

A whole world of love and gentleness was contained in those few words of hers.

And when he began to talk to Mrs. White, first about the weather and then about Rosebud herself, Childie in the pride of her heart thought he looked quite the gentleman, every inch the gentleman, although there was scarcely an inch of his coat which was not shabby and shiny. Still, that did not matter; he had gentle, courteous manners, which are more becoming than fine clothes.

"Grand-dad," said Childie as they were starting, "you'll take care of the shop and of your own dear old self, won't you? And I shall be back to give you your dinner, grand-dad. And *do* use both your eyes when you read; and don't trouble to dust the books, grand-dad dear, for I'll do all that this afternoon. And say something kind to Jane Eyre and Robinson Crusoe, for they'll be lonely without me. Good-bye, dear."

"Good-bye, Childie," he answered. "I think I shall be lonely too; so Jane Eyre and Robinson Crusoe and I will comfort each other."

When they had gone—and their departure was witnessed by Mr. Jones, who stood at his door waving his hat frantically—when they had gone, grand-dad pulled out that red cotton handkerchief, and removed from his face several curious little tears which were having a race down his thin old cheeks.

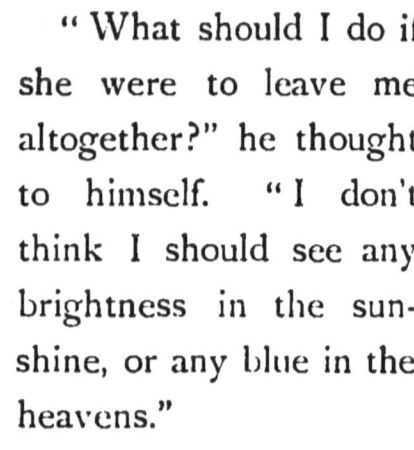

"What should I do if she were to leave me altogether?" he thought to himself. "I don't think I should see any brightness in the sunshine, or any blue in the heavens."

Perhaps you, too, will think him rather a silly old man; but you must remember that Childie was all in all to him, and that he had learnt to look upon her as his friend and companion, yes, almost as his little mother.

He found her dolls in a corner of the shop. He lifted them up very tenderly, and examined Mr.

Crusoe's squashed arm. He did not know much about medicine, but he dressed the arm as well as he could; and no doubt Crusoe would have thanked him if he had had a tongue in his mouth.

"Childie says you are to spend the morning with me," he said to them solemnly, just as if they were real persons.

He put them both on her stool, which he placed near his own arm-chair; and taking up a learnèd book became deeply engrossed in it, stopping now and again to have a pinch of that horrid snuff. But, sorrowful to relate, he forgot all about Childie's injunction, and he closed his right eye with the second finger of his right hand and read with his left eye!

Meanwhile Rosebud and Mrs. White were creeping slowly towards Grosvenor Square. Rosebud herself could have been there and back six times over; but Mrs. White was not able to get along very fast, for she was heavy, and so was that mantle of hers, and that wonderful bonnet with the violet tuft! But at last they arrived, and Childie stood gazing in awe at the great big solemn house.

"I suppose, ma'am," she said, "the tall gentleman must have a very large family to have such a very large house?"

Mrs. White laughed.

"Bless you, no!" she answered. "He's only got Miss Violet."

"If you please, ma'am," said Childie timidly, as they rang at the bell and waited to be admitted; "if you please, ma'am, I'm rather frightened. I've never been to such a grand place before. Ours isn't so grand, is it?"

"Not quite," replied Mrs. White smiling, and giving the child an encouraging nod. "But don't you be frightened, for I'm going to be your friend, you know. And let me tell you, deary, that it is something to have Mrs. Rebecca White as a friend."

The footman opened the door. Mrs. White bade Childie follow her, and took her up some stairs which led to the first floor. The landing was covered with beautiful rich velvet carpet. The whole place seemed to Childie like fairy-land. There were huge vases with bulrushes in them, and shining brass ornaments on brackets, and curious spears and swords and costly plates of many different colours and shapes fastened on to the wall. Childie was quite bewildered at everything, for she had been accustomed only to the sight of shabby second-hand books all her little life.

"Here we are," said Mrs. White cheerily, pointing to a door. "That's Miss Violet's boudoir. You knock and go in bravely by yourself. There'll be no one but her. And she's quite looking forward to seeing you. She don't want to see me."

Childie's heart beat very fast as she knocked timidly at the door. A voice cried:

"Come in!"

Then Childie opened the door just wide enough for her to slip through, and still holding on to the handle, she made a little curtsy and said:

"If you please, miss, I've come."

CHAPTER V.

VIOLET AND ROSEBUD.

Violet's sofa was placed so that she could see anyone coming into the room. Her face brightened up at the sight of Childie's dear quaint little figure. She held out her hand in kindly welcome.

"I am very pleased you have come, Rosebud," she said, smiling brightly. "Mrs. White has put a chair for you by my side. You will sit down. won't you, and take your hat and cape off?"

There was something so friendly in her manner that Childie lost all sense of nervousness.

"I am so glad to see you, miss," she said earnestly. "Ever since the tall gentleman, your papa, spoke of you, I've been thinking, oh! such a lot about you."

"That is very sweet of you," said Violet gently. "Move your chair a little closer to me, will you?"

Childie drew it nearer to the sofa, and Violet took her hand and kept it prisoner.

"I am feeling much better to-day," she said brightly. "Do you know, the doctors promise that in time I shall be quite strong—like you are. But it seems too good to be true."

"Oh, but it will be true!" cried Childe eagerly. "One must always go on hoping. That is what I say to grand-dad when he is sad and anxious. It makes all the difference in the world if one has hope, doesn't it?"

"I think it does," answered Violet. "I shall remember what you say. Papa tells me you have read a great many books, and that you are very wise; so you must teach me to be wise."

Childie laughed.

"I am sure I couldn't do that," she said, "because I am not wise myself. Grand-dad's the one to know a lot. He *does* know a lot. He is a walking library. Oh! you would like him, I am sure. And then there's Mr. Jones. He is not clever about books, but there is no one in the world that knows more about birds than he does. He has all the names on the tip of his tongue. And he has the most wonderful parrot, whom he has taught to say 'Things will take a turn '."

"I should like to hear him say that," cried Violet.

"He says it about a thousand times every day," laughed Childie. "Mr. Jones declares we can't hear it too often. Mr. Jones has taught him other things too; and I believe he is teaching him something quite new, but I don't know what it is yet."

And then Childie told Violet all about the birds in Mr. Jones's shop, not forgetting the little piping bullfinch. Now and again she stopped, but Violet always said:

"Do go on, Rosebud, if you're not tired; for don't think I am tired of listening."

And then somehow or other they got on the subject of dolls, and Childie gave her an account of Jane Eyre and Robinson Crusoe, not mentioning, however, the terrible accident which had deprived Mr. Crusoe of the use of his right arm.

"Are both your dolls in good health?" asked Violet slyly.

"Oh! pretty good," answered Childie cheerfully, "considering the sudden heat, you know. That seems to try every one. The lady who came to fetch me this morning was quite tired out."

"Rosebud," said Violet suddenly, "I know one of your dolls is not in good health. I always find out papa's secrets. Now, here is a doll I want you very much to have. I made a hat for it last night."

She took from beneath the coverlet a most gorgeously-dressed doll-individual.

"For me?" cried Childie aghast. In her wildest dreams she had never imagined to herself such a doll as this.

"Yes, for you," answered Violet, delighted to see her surprise and enjoyment.

"May I kiss you?" asked Childie, her little face flushed with excitement and gratitude.

It was not the doll she cared so much about as the kindness.

"Yes; please kiss me," said Violet.

And Childie bent over and kissed the little girl tenderly.

"I could love you so much if you would let me," she whispered.

"Do love me," answered Violet, whose face shone with a bright smile.

And this was the sweet beginning of their friendship.

"What are you going to call that doll?" asked Violet. "You always choose odd names for your dolls, don't you?"

"I think I shall call her Queen Elizabeth," laughed Childie, "or Marie Antoinette. Which do you prefer?"

"One of them lost her head," said Violet. "I'd choose the name of the person who did not lose her head?"

"That would be Queen Elizabeth, then," replied Childie; "although I read in a book the other day that she too lost her head. But grand-dad explained to me that it only meant she became confused and didn't know what she was doing. I was very puzzled at the time, but I think I understand now. Grand-dad says a great many kings and queens have lost their heads—in both senses, you know!"

Then they talked about books, and Childie was quite distressed that some of Violet's beautiful books did not wear brown-paper overcoats.

"Will you let me cover them?" she said with

motherly anxiety. "You don't know how clever I am at covering books. But at home I cut out the over-coats to hide the shabbiness of our books; here I should make them to protect the beautiful binding."

"You shall cover one now," said Violet laughing. "Here is the brown paper that Queen Elizabeth came in, and here is a pair of scissors, and there is a book that ought to have a cover."

And thus the morning sped away; and Mrs. White arrived with some tempting cake, and found the two little girls in happy and eager conversation.

"You don't look very frightened now, child," she said kindly.

"No, ma'am," answered Rosebud with a bright, frank smile; "I'm not at all frightened now. Only I hope I have not tired the little lady."

"Indeed she has not!" cried Violet. "I've been so happy, Mrs. White, and the time has passed only too quickly. I don't often say that, do I, Mrs. White?" she asked somewhat sadly.

"No, deary," answered Mrs. White. "But you're going to begin to say it; that I'm sure of. Ah! here's the master."

"I'm so glad you'll see papa before you go," said Violet, turning to Childie, who was putting on her hat and cape. "Papa dear, Rosebud has made me very happy."

"Ah! I knew she would," said Mr. Dighton, sitting down on Violet's sofa, and holding out his hand to Childie, who smiled with delight to see him, for he was a sort of tall hero to her. "Thank you, Rosebud, for making my little girl happy. Now you are going home to your grandfather, and you must remember to tell him that we shall want him to spare you for a short time every day, either in the morning or the afternoon, whichever is best for you."

"Please, sir," answered Childie, "I should prefer to come in the afternoon, because grand-dad likes to go out in the morning. And," she added quaintly, "I always feel a little anxious when he goes out in the afternoon and does not come home

"THANK YOU, ROSEBUD, FOR MAKING MY LITTLE GIRL HAPPY."

until dusk; for he is old now, and his eyesight is bad, and he can't get over the crossings very quickly."

"Very well, little Rosebud," he said kindly; "you shall come in the afternoons. Now, good-bye, little junior partner. By the way, how is Mr. Crusoe? Is his arm to be cut off?"

"The doctors cannot tell me yet," she laughed —for she enjoyed a bit of a joke—" but I do not think Mr. Crusoe will take any harm!"

"What a good thing it is," said Mr. Dighton solemnly, "that you are going to earn a little money every week, for you will be able to give Mr. Crusoe a few luxuries now that he is ill."

"No," said Childie, laughing again. "I shall keep the luxuries for Queen Elizabeth. The little lady has given her to me, and I shall take every care of her. Only I don't see that I deserve to have such a beautiful present. I can't think what grand-dad and Mr. Jones will say. They will be surprised."

"Oh, papa," cried Violet, "mayn't I have the

piping bullfinch from Mr. Jones's shop? I'd nearly forgotten to ask you."

"Of course you shall, dear," he answered, glad to please her in anything and everything. "Rosebud shall bring it with her to-morrow afternoon; or, better still, we'll send the footman to fetch it."

"Oh, thank you," said Childie, tears of delight glistening in her eyes. "That *is* kind of you. And I shall be *so* proud to tell Mr. Jones."

Her little hands were clasped together tightly; her face beamed with happiness.

"He is so good to me," she said earnestly. "You can't think how kind he is. And I know he will be pleased to hear you are going to buy the bullfinch."

She said good-bye to her new friends; and one and all were pleased to have seen her. Even the footman, James, condescended to give her a smile. And this was very extraordinary; for he generally frowned at people, or glared at them, especially if they were inconsiderate enough to trouble him to answer the front bell, when he was enjoying his newspaper or his tea!

Childie went on her way home, thinking first of the little delicate lady, then of the tall gentleman, then of Mrs. White, then of Queen Elizabeth, then of the footman with the stiff neck, and last, not least, of grand-dad and Mr. Jones. She had made many new friends, and seen many beautiful things, but her heart was faithful to the old friends and the old familiar things she loved.

"The house may be very grand," she said to herself, "but it's not like our book-shop. There may be many beautiful ornaments about, but I don't care for them as much as for our dear second-hand books. And those stuffed birds under the glass case! Why, Mr. Jones has real birds, and of course they are better than stuffed ones!"

She could not resist running into Mr. Jones's shop just to tell him the good news.

"Mr. Jones!" she cried. "I can't wait because grand-dad will be wanting his dinner, but I've sold your piping bullfinch for you, and the footman is coming to fetch it to-morrow. Mr. Jones, I'm so glad, aren't you?"

Mr. Jones made no answer, but catching hold of both her hands, whirled her round and round, until she called out to him to stop.

CHAPTER VI.

THE WONDERFUL PARROT.

So the junior partner of the second-hand bookshop went backwards and forwards to the grand house in Grosvenor Square. Every afternoon at two o'clock she said good-bye to grand-dad, Queen Elizabeth, Jane Eyre, Mr. Crusoe, and Mr. Jones, and hurried off to business.

"Ain't you just proud of yourself, Birdie?" said Mr. Jones one afternoon, as she passed by his shop and gave him her usual greeting. "Ain't you just proud of helping grand-dad? There now, I should be! What I like about you, Rosebud child, is that you don't alter to your old friends. That's saying a good deal, you know, in this 'ere queerish world."

"You don't mean to say that people do forget their old friends?" asked Childie, much shocked.

Mr. Jones nodded his head violently.

"I mean what I say," he remarked gravely. "But there now, don't you take no heed of me. Time enough to think about these things when you're old and ugly like I am."

"You're not ugly, I'm sure!" laughed Childie. "Of course there is one little bit of your face which is not pretty, Mr. Jones. But I don't think I'd even have that altered. You wouldn't be my Mr. Jones unless you had a red nose."

"Ah," he answered, "I guessed it was my nose you were finding fault with. You're always poking fun at my nose."

"Indeed, Mr. Jones," she laughed, fondling his rough old hand, "I'm very fond of your nose! Mr. Jones, I want you to give a look-in to granddad this afternoon, will you? I think he is rather lonely sometimes; and of course I am obliged to go out every afternoon. Business must be done regularly, mustn't it?"

Mr. Jones smiled at the little business-woman standing before him.

"Quite right, Childie," he answered. "Stick to your work like a man."

"It is very pleasant business," she continued. "I feel perfectly at home there now, and Miss Violet seems to get stronger and brighter every day. She says it is all through me; but I don't see how that can be, for I'm not a doctor. I thought only doctors could make people well."

"Ain't you a doctor?" asked Mr. Jones. "Well, I don't know who is a doctor if you ain't one. Don't you doctor up them sick books, and granddad, and your humble servant, and your humble servant's torn coats? Why, if I'm just feeling in the blues, don't I come to you for physic, and you give it me? Ain't kind words and bright smiles physic? Ain't they or ain't they not, Birdie?"

"I'm sure I don't know," laughed Childie. "And that reminds me, Mr. Jones, the bullfinch is not feeling very well."

"Too many hemp seeds, Rosebud, too many

hemp seeds!" said Mr. Jones, trying to look very stern and failing utterly. "Cut them off!"

"Do you think, Mr. Jones," asked Childie timidly, "that you could find time to come and see the bird yourself? Miss Violet would be so grateful to you, and I should too."

Mr. Jones stroked his chin thoughtfully.

"It ain't much in my line," he answered, "to visit them grand places; but I don't mind making an exception in your favour, Rosebud. Only it's the stout person as came to fetch you that I'm thinking of. She's awful proud and haughty. And I'm frightened of her. That's the plain truth, Childie."

"I will take care of you, Mr. Jones," said Childie smiling. "And you know she is really very nice. It's wonderful how nice people are when you come to know them."

"Are they now?" asked Mr. Jones doubtfully.

"Well, I daresay you're right, Rosebud. Anyway, I'll come to have a look at the bullfinch. Name your time, and see if I'm not ready. And now off you go to your business. And keep your mind easy about the grand-dad, for I'll pop in to see him."

Then Childie went on her way to Grosvenor Square, and Mr. Jones retired into his shop, muttering to himself these mysterious words:

"Won't that 'ere child be just took aback when she hears the parrot saying her new lines!"

He then chuckled several times, for reasons best known to himself, and turning up his shirt sleeves as he always did when he was about to undertake a tough piece of work, he sat on a stool and addressed his favourite parrot thus:

"Now, old Donkey, I'm just going on with our bit of schooling. And hark you, if you've forgotten them new words, I'll crack your little skull for you, that I will. Do you hear, old screecher?

"Things 'ave took a turn—'urrah! Things 'ave took a turn—'urrah! Say that, Donkey."

With wonderful patience Mr. Jones repeated these words a fearful number of times, until he was really quite exhausted with the terrible exertion.

The parrot remained perfectly mute, but put her head on one side and rolled her eyes in a very knowing manner. She was taking it all in. But not one little word did she vouchsafe; and Mr. Jones, having devoted a long time to her education, left her to meditate on the lesson, and ran over to the second-hand book-shop to smoke a pipe with grand-dad.

Grand-dad, as usual, was reading a very learnèd book, which he put aside when the bird-fancier entered.

"I'm glad to see you, Mr. Jones," he said smiling, and pointing to a chair.

"Thank you, sir, I'm sure," answered Mr. Jones.

He always called grand-dad "sir", for he had an immense respect and admiration for the quiet, white-haired, scholarly gentleman.

"I was feeling a wee bit lonely, sir," he continued, as he lit his pipe and offered the match to grand-dad, "and I thought as I'd just come over for a smoke and a chat. The street seems queerish without the littl'un; don't it, sir?"

"Yes, it does," answered grand-dad, his face brightening up as he thought of Childie. "But I'm glad she should have the change, Mr. Jones, for it must be dull work along with me, you know."

"Well, she don't seem to find it so," said Mr. Jones earnestly. "Rosebud is never so happy as when she is sitting by your side reading, or doing her bit of stitching. Why, to speak plain, I'm sometimes an inch or two jealous of you."

Grand-dad smiled and said gently:

"I am quite certain you need not be jealous, for Childie loves you very dearly, Mr. Jones; and indeed she ought to do so, since you are our kind faithful friend. I do not say much about it, but you must believe that I am grateful to you, will you not?"

He leaned forward and held out his hand, which Mr. Jones grasped heartily.

"Thank you, sir," he said, rubbing his eyes across his coat-sleeves; "thank you for them words. I'm just as proud as a peacock to hear you call me a friend. Bless me, how I've watched that littl'un growing up! And every day I said to myself she's grown a bit taller and a bit beautifuller. Ain't I just proud of her now! There's no one in Grosvenor Square like our Rosebud, sir. Grosvenor Square, indeed!"

"There's no one in the whole world like Childie," answered grand-dad lovingly. " I think she is one of God's own gracious smiles."

At that moment a very learnèd-looking lady, with a stern face and a pair of stern spectacles, came into the shop and asked for a book, the very name of which frightened Mr. Jones out of his seven senses. Nodding kindly to Jane Eyre, Robinson Crusoe, and Queen Elizabeth, who were, as usual, reposing on a chair by grand-dad's side, Mr. Jones fled away, thinking to himself what a good thing it was that birds had not such long names as books.

" I should be floored," he said, "for I'm nothing of a scholar, nothing at all."

He crossed the road and made for his shop, and as he neared it he heard some wonderful sounds which caused his red nose to become redder than ever, and his heart to beat violently with excitement.

The parrot, sly bird! had learnt her lesson an was screeching at the top of her voice:

"Things 'ave took a turn! things 'ave took a turn—'urrah! Say that, Donkey!"

CHAPTER VII.

MR. JONES VISITS GROSVENOR SQUARE.

Childie had confided to Violet Mr. Jones's fear of Mrs. White.

"Oh, we'll look after him, Rosebud," Violet had answered encouragingly. "You tell him from me that there is nothing at all to be afraid of, and that I am sure Mrs. White will be very kind to him."

All the same, she took the precaution of getting Mrs. White into a very good temper on the afternoon when Mr. Jones was to accompany Rosebud to Grosvenor Square. She took her medicine without a minute's hesitation; and she was so bright and cheerful that Mrs. White, who loved her little mistress dearly, smiled with delight to think she was really becoming stronger.

"You've changed wonderful these last few weeks, deary," she said affectionately. "Why, there's a colour on your face, and you look happier. You'll soon be getting about and running faster than I can. It's all along of that Rosebud. Bless her dear little heart! Never shall I forget the day when I went to fetch her, and she, seeing me looking tired and hot, took a paper and fanned me so nicely. She's got a wonderful way about her, Miss Violet. There's not a soul in the house that doesn't love her. Even James smiles pleasant when he sees her coming; and that's saying a good deal, because he generally looks awful cross and disagreeable."

"I am so glad you love Rosebud," said Violet eagerly. "I can't tell you how I love her, dear Mrs. White. I don't know what I should do if she could not come to me every day. She has always such a lot to tell me about her grandfather and about her friend, Mr. Jones. I am quite anxious to see them both. I am sorry not to have seen her grandfather when he came the other morning to look at papa's library. But he will come again soon, and then I shall tell him how I love Rosebud."

"*He* is the real gentleman," answered Mrs. White. "I know them when I see them. But, deary me, Mr. Jones!—well, he's a different sort."

"He must be very nice for Rosebud to love him," said Violet staunchly. "You've got the bullfinch ready, haven't you, dear Mrs. White? for you remember that Mr. Jones is coming this afternoon. And you'll find him a cup of tea, won't you? I daresay he will be tired after his long walk."

She looked up pleadingly, for she was very anxious to make everything pleasant for Rosebud's great friend.

Mrs. White understood the look.

"Bless your heart, deary!" she said affectionately, "I'm going to be kind to the bird-fancier for your sake, and for Rosebud's sake too. He shall have tea enough for ten; so don't you worry your little self. Here they come, Miss Violet: I can hear Rosebud's voice. I'll just go and meet them on the landing and say something nice; and then when you want me, deary, I'll come and serve the tea for you. You'd like him to have his cup of tea along with you this afternoon, wouldn't you?"

"Thank you, dear Mrs. White," she answered gratefully. "I should like that very much."

Mrs. White trundled off to give a kindly greeting to Mr. Jones, who, by the way, quite forgot to take off his hat when he saw her, and became very confused and nervous, and held Rosebud's hand very tightly; for he believed thoroughly in her protecting care.

"I am pleased to see you," said Mrs. White benignly.

"Same to you, ma'am," answered Mr. Jones in a melancholy tone of voice.

"It is a warm afternoon, Mr. Jones, isn't it?" continued Mrs. White kindly.

"Shockin' 'ot," he said, puffing rather violently, and then taking out his handkerchief and wiping his face.

"You will find Miss Violet in her room," said Mrs. White, smiling in a most friendly manner. "She is anxiously waiting for her friends; and I daresay you'll be glad of a cup of tea soon, Mr. Jones?"

"Right you are, ma'am," he answered, gaining confidence.

And when she had passed on her way downstairs, Mr. Jones, stooping down, whispered to Childie:

"I say, littl'un, this polite business is harder work than cleaning the whole blessèd shop out. How did I bear myself to that 'ere party?"

"Very nicely indeed, dear Mr. Jones," she said. "I'm sure I'm quite proud of you!"

"She don't look near so frightening without that haughty black bonnet concern on her old head," he remarked, as he took his hat off and put it under his arm.

"Didn't I tell you she was very kind?" answered Childie. "Oh, but I do wonder what you'll think of dear Miss Violet, Mr. Jones. If you don't love her the very first minute you see her, I'll never speak to you again."

She knocked at Violet's boudoir-door and went in, leading Mr. Jones by the right hand.

"If you please, dear Miss Violet," she said, bringing her companion up to Violet's sofa, "this is my friend, Mr. Jones."

The little lady on the sofa smiled her brightest, and shook hands with Rosebud's great friend.

"I'm pleased to make your acquaintance," he said cheerily, for he had quite recovered his composure now. "I've heard a sight about you from the littl'un, and I make bold to say I knows you quite familiarlike."

"And I am sure I know all about you, Mr. Jones," laughed Violet; "for Rosebud is always saying nice things about you, and I am just longing to come and see your shop. Rosebud has given me a lovely description of all your beautiful birds. I know which one I should choose to buy next."

"And which might that be?" asked Mr. Jones.

"Why, of course, the parrot," said Violet.

"Oh, the parrot, to be sure!" replied Mr. Jones, and went into fits of laughter at some private joke of his own. "Ah, she's a 'cute bird that, although

she's only had a governess at home, and ain't been to no grand school, and ain't learned out of no second-hand books from that 'ere child's grand-dad's shop. But she knows a thing or two, she do, and she don't forget."

Rosebud, seeing that the two were getting on

well together, went out of the room to fetch her work, and then Mr. Jones nudged Violet and said confidingly:

"You'll have to come and hear that parrot speak her *new lines*. When I heard her last evening I thought I should have burst with joy, because I'd taken a deal of trouble with schooling her. And all she did was to roll her little eyes, and put her little head on one side like this, you know, until I felt that aggravated I could have wrung her obstinate neck. But in the evening she said it pat off, plainer than any human being; as nice as you or I might speak."

"And what was it she said?" asked Violet eagerly.

"Well, I'm not sure as I'll tell you," he answered; then, seeing her look of disappointment, he added:

"Yes, I will, missy, only don't you go telling the littl'un, because I want her to hear for her dear little self."

Then he told the story to Violet, and she clapped

her hands with delight, and of course longed to give this piece of news to Childie.

"Won't Rosebud laugh!" she said, smiling at him.

"Won't she just?" he answered proudly. "You know, last night I hoped that bird would speak up when Rosebud came in to brush up my things, and make them look a bit fresh for to come and see you in. And she brought this blue neck-tie, and told me as I was to wear it to-day. A pretty thing, ain't it? Not the same style as your sash, but wonderful sweet of its kind."

"Very pretty," said Violet, glancing at it.

"Oh, bless your heart! She has good taste, she has," he replied, stroking his red nose. "She's a clever little party, is Childie. She's got more learning in her finger-nail than you or me has got in our whole bodies. But that's neither here nor there; what I looks to is her goodness; and I ain't got fine words to speak about that. But don't I just feel, missy, don't I just feel. That's all."

"I am sure you do," answered Violet earnestly, putting her little delicate hand on his arm, "and I do too, Mr. Jones; for Rosebud is like a little mother to me, and I love her more and more every day."

Mr. Jones listened delightedly whilst she spoke of Childie, nodding his bald head approvingly and smiling very proudly. And then, when she had finished, and he saw the tears of eagerness in her eyes, he took her little hand and put it very gently and respectfully to his lips.

"I'm just blessed if Rosebud or anyone else could keep themselves from loving you, dear little missy," he said kindly. "And I'm proud to see you, I am. And when you take to running about, and come to my shop, won't I just give you a welcome—trust me!"

"Thank you," said Violet. "And oh, Mr. Jones, what about the bullfinch? Rosebud and I have been quite anxious about it, haven't we, Rosebud?" she added, as Childie came into the room, carrying her work-basket in one hand and some brown paper in another; for she was going to cover a new book which Mr. Dighton had brought home for Violet the previous night.

"Yes, indeed, we've been quite anxious," said Childie. "But Mr. Jones laughs at our fears, and declares we've given the bird too many hemp seeds. But he always says that just to tease me, I believe."

"None of your poking fun at me," said Mr. Jones, shaking his fist at her. "You don't know nothing about birds, you don't. That's my line of business. You go on with your stitching or what not, whilst I have a peep at the bullfinch. Ah!" he exclaimed, as he looked at the bird, "what a beauty it is! Did you ever see the like of the breast, and the wee bright black eyes, and the sly little head? The finest bullfinch in the whole world! And can't he just sing as loud as any trumpet? He's all right enough, except for them hemp seeds. They make him feel heavy-like. Cut them off! I'm proud, missy, that I sold you this 'ere bird, for I declare he's a downright credit to you and to me too."

"I am very glad to have him," said Violet smiling. "He is quite a companion in the mornings. And, do you know, he always sings directly Rosebud comes into the room."

"Of course he does," answered Mr. Jones. "He thinks she's the sunshine, he do. He's a knowing bird. But not like the parrot, bless me, not like the parrot!"

Childie was busy cutting out a brown paper overcoat for the new book, and did not see Mr. Jones and Violet smiling mysteriously at each other.

She was very happy that they had made friends together; for of course it was a responsibility for her to introduce her friend to strange people, who did not know his funny ways and his kind heart. And it would have been very disappointing to her if Violet had not taken kindly to him.

As for him, he was really in capital spirits, and seemed quite at ease in the grand room.

"Nice, tidy, pretty room this is, to be sure!" he remarked, "and what remarkable fine pictures. They remind me rather of some my old grandmother had as belonged to her mother, sweet, pretty things! And so you lie here all the day long and look at them, missy?"

"Yes; but I am going to walk soon, am I not,

Rosebud dear?" said Violet, turning lovingly to her little mother.

"Yes, indeed you are, dear Miss Violet," she answered. "That will be a happy day, won't it?"

At least that was a happy afternoon. Mrs. White joined the company, and was graciousness itself to Mr. Jones, although in her heart of hearts she considered he was rather a queer sort of person, certainly not the usual kind of visitor at No. 12, Grosvenor Square. And then he looked rather odd too: his coat, black broadcloth, was certainly well brushed, but it was very shiny and greasy, and somewhat tight for him—he was not a slim individual! His boots, which he had taken a tremendous long time to polish, were not particularly elegant, and there was no denying that his nose was very red and his head very bald. But in spite of nose, and head, and boots, and coat, Mrs. White was *inclined* to like him. When James the footman brought the tea-tray in, holding *his* nose rather high, because he felt rather aggrieved at having to wait upon this kind of visitor, Mrs. White ordered him about very sternly, and his nose came down with a leap, for it was not wise to displease or annoy Mrs. White.

Mr. Jones had partaken of the bulk of the tea-cake and a portion of Swiss roll, which he called "a wonderful relish", and several cups of tea, which he said were "prime", and half a dozen or so thin slices of bread-and-butter, which he declared were "juicy little mouthfuls", and was resting from his exertions, when the door opened and Mr. Dighton came in.

"Ah, I'm disturbing a tea-party," he said smiling kindly. "Well, Rosebud, and is this your friend, Mr. Jones? I am pleased to see you, Mr. Jones. Can you speak with me a minute?"

Mr. Jones followed Mr. Dighton out of the room, wondering what on earth the gentleman could have to say to him.

"At your service, sir," he said, as they stood together on the landing.

"Well, it is just this, Mr. Jones," said Mr. Dighton quietly. "I have been calling at Mr. Burnley's shop to make some proposals to him about my library, which sadly wants putting in order; and to my grief I found he was ill. He had fainted away in his chair. I called in help and we brought him to, and when he opened his eyes he murmured: 'Childie, where is Childie?' So I left him in charge of a neighbour, and hurried on here. Now, shall I tell Rosebud, or will you? I fear the old man is going to be very ill. He looks as pale as death."

"I'll tell her," said Mr. Jones. "Rosebud is as brave as a lion; she'll keep quiet, you see."

He went straight back to the room, and himself tried hard to keep calm.

"Littl'un," he said very tenderly, "grand-dad's not feeling particularly well, and wants you to come home to him; just to look after him, you know, Childie."

Her face turned pale, her lips quivered slightly; her loving heart was full of sadness to think that grand-dad was ill and she was not by his side. She gathered together her things, hastily kissed Violet and Mrs. White, smiled sadly at Mr. Dighton, who stood in the doorway and whispered:

"Good little Rosebud, keep up a brave heart."

And clinging close to Mr. Jones she passed silently down the endless stairs, through the long passage, and out into the street.

"Grand-dad is ill and I am not by his side."

was all she said; but there was a whole world of sorrow in those few words.

"The way seems twelve times longer than sual," she sighed, when they had nearly arrived at the book-shop.

"Courage, Childie," said Mr. Jones cheerily; "just a few yards more, and you'll be with grand-dad."

And in two or three minutes Childie was kneeling by grand-dad's side, kissing his dear hands and his dear face.

"Grand-dad, darling," she whispered, "Childie has come, and will never leave you again."

"THE DOCTOR CAME TO SEE HIM AND LOOKED GRAVE."

CHAPTER VIII.

A CHAPTER OF PLEASANT SURPRISES.

Grand-dad was very ill. Mr. Dighton's own doctor came to see him, and looked grave. He had taken a bad chill, and he had to fight against old age.

"Who is going to nurse him?" asked the doctor of Childie.

"If you please, sir," answered Childie, "I am going to nurse him. But if you don't think I know enough, sir, I shall be quite content so long as I am in the room all the time, just to be near him if he wants me. But I'll take such care of him, and Mr. Jones will help me."

"I'm sure you will take care of him," said the doctor kindly. "Well, we shall see to-morrow whether you can manage alone."

It was a sadly anxious time for Childie; but if the kindness of friends can be any consolation in the hour of trouble, then indeed Childie must have had great consolation. For Mrs. White arrived, bringing loving messages from Violet and some few delicacies for grand-dad; and, dear old soul that she was, she wouldn't hear of going home that night, but kept watch with Childie in grand-dad's room, and looked after Childie and made her take food and tea, and spoke kind cheering words to her.

"Don't you fear, deary, that I'm going to forget you now you want help," she said to Rose-bud. "And do you think, deary, as how I could get a wink of sleep if you were sitting up alone with your poor, dear grandfather? No, here's my place, and here I'm going to be; and if master had refused me, I'd have come all the same. But he was only too glad to have me come, bless his kind heart."

The next morning, as Mrs. White was leaving the book-shop just to go and see after Violet, Mr.

Jones, laden with a large bunch of pinks and cornflowers, which he had brought all the way from Covent Garden, stopped her and begged her to take them to Childie.

"I've never been sick myself," he said, "but I've heard as sick folk like a whole sight of flowers in their rooms; and so I thought as I'd just buy these 'ere bunches to make the place look cheerful. Begging your pardon for troubling you, ma'am, but I should feel very grateful if you'd pop them into Childie's little hands. I don't like to run up myself, for fear of creaking with these heavy boots of mine."

"Do you know, you are very kind, Mr. Jones?" said Mrs. White, taking the flowers from him. "I think you are a most kind person."

"Why now, ma'am," he answered, "I do believe you're making fun of me, like Rosebud do sometimes. Poor little dear thing! Ain't she got a brave heart, ma'am? How I think of her in her trouble! And there's very little work I can do now. Last night a customer came in and wanted a linnet. He could have had the whole lot for all I cared, cages and seed and all, and I'd never have asked him for no money in return.

But there now, ma'am, begging your pardon for keeping you standing, I'm sure."

In the afternoon, when Mrs. White returned, she found him in the shop, dusting the books in a melancholy kind of manner.

"I thought as I must do something," he said sadly. "Men is no good in a sick-room; and I just knew Childie would be pleased if I gave a dust to the grand-dad's books. He and she think a deal of them, they do. And Childie's mighty particular about them."

Mrs. White was touched by his forlorn condition.

"Look you," she said kindly, "I'll come down and finish dusting the books, and you shall go up and sit quietly for an hour with Rosebud, and she'll tell you how pleased she was with the beautiful flowers."

And she was true to her word, for she came down in about a quarter of an hour; and Mr. Jones, slipping off his boots, crept upstairs, taking with him Jane Eyre, Robinson Crusoe, and Queen Elizabeth, whom he had found neglected and forgotten in a corner of the shop.

"They're only dolls," he said to himself; "but they're part of the family household, and maybe they'll gladden the littl'un."

But *he* gladdened her still more, sitting quietly by her side holding her hand.

"Ain't you going to be a clever little doctor?" he whispered as he watched her give grand-dad some medicine. "Ain't you going to cure grand-dad quickly? Why, to be sure, you're cleverer than twenty of them old stupids as drives about in their fine carriages, and calls at the houses, and looks awful solemn and haughty. Our Rosebud is the doctor for us."

But she shook her head and whispered in return:

"Mr. Jones dear, they say he is very ill; and of course he's old too, and hasn't the strength that I have. I wish I could give him mine."

"She ain't got much to give," thought Mr. Jones as he looked at Rosebud's sad anxious little face.

And so the weary days passed away, and sometimes grand-dad was better and sometimes worse. Mrs. White came every day, and kind Mr. Dighton was always calling in, bringing letters and

messages from Violet; and even James, the footman with the stiff neck, came one evening quite on his own account to inquire after Rosebud's grand-dad.

"Did you ever hear the like?" said Mrs. White

when she heard of James's visit. "I'd have sooner thought of one of Madame Tussaud's figures leaving the wax-work room and coming here to pay a friendly call!"

There was one little lady who was longing to come and see Childie, and put her arms round her and kiss her. She had not been very well for the last few days, for she was but a fragile, delicate little flower; and she was full of grief for Rosebud's sake, and felt herself quite lost without her little mother's affectionate companionship.

One morning she said to Mr. Dighton:

"Papa, dear, will you take me to see Rosebud to-day?"

It was the first time she had ever proposed to go out. The doctors had told Mr. Dighton repeatedly that if she could once make the effort she would become all the stronger, and that she would soon learn to have confidence in her strength, and that confidence would bring more strength.

Mr. Dighton was overjoyed at her request.

"That is my brave little girl!" he said, fondling her fair hair. "Of course I will take you to see Rosebud. We will go quite by ourselves, and we won't even tell Mrs. White our secret, so that she will be just as surprised as Rosebud. Hurrah! little Violet, you will see Rosebud again, and her quaint old home, and Mr. Jones perhaps; and, who knows, we may be able to pay a visit to his shop. But what you will like best of all, Violet, is that you will cheer Rosebud, and bid her take hope and comfort for her poor old grandfather."

"Yes, indeed, I will," she answered earnestly. "She has been so much to me, papa dear, and I want to be something to her."

When Mrs. White was safely out of the house Mr. Dighton ordered James to get Violet's bath-chair in readiness. He had bought it ever so long ago in the hopes that she would be persuaded to use it.

"We shall not want you, James," said Mr. Dighton, "because I myself am going to wheel it."

James stared, and thought the world was coming to an end; but he did not dare to ask any questions.

Then Violet was dressed, and Mr. Dighton carried her tenderly downstairs, looking very happy; for he loved his little girl with all the love of his kind heart, and it seemed to him that the future was going to be very bright for her and for him. There was nothing to cloud his happiness, except, indeed, grand-dad's illness; and he had wonderful schemes in his mind for Rosebud and her grandfather when he should have recovered his health and strength.

He chatted cheerily to Violet as he wheeled her along.

"Tell me if I bump you too much," he said.

"You don't bump me at all," she said, smiling happily. "And what a lovely morning it is, papa dear! Doesn't it seem sad that anyone should be ill on such a beautiful warm day?"

She was not at all nervous, although this was the first time she had been out in her chair. Her one thought was to get to Rosebud.

At last they turned down the narrow street and stopped in front of a tumble-down old second-hand book-shop.

"Here we are!" said Mr. Dighton. "This is Rosebud's home. Now, little lady, shall I carry you in, or are you going to step out for yourself?"

"I am going to step out for myself," she said, trembling with eagerness.

And with the help of his strong hand she walked into the book-shop.

But she had been observed by a certain red-nosed person on the other side of the road. He flew across and arrived just in time to get grand-dad's arm-chair ready for her.

"Well now!" he said excitedly, "this is just pretty of you, it is! Who'd have thought as how the little lady would have come here so soon. God bless her little heart!"

Without any ceremony at all he snatched a cushion from Mr. Dighton and arranged it nicely for Violet, and, seizing the biggest book he could find, placed her little feet upon it, all the time murmuring:

"This is just pretty of you, it is. Ain't I just pleased too, that's all!"

He then remembered the existence of Mr. Dighton, who had stood watching his thoughtful attentions.

"Begging your pardon, sir," he sad politely, "but I was so excited to see the little lady that I'm blessed if I didn't forget yourself. Please be seated, sir; and make yourself at home, I'm sure, while I go and tell Rosebud as some folks is wanting to see her. She is a bit easier to-day, sir; for the grand-dad's had a good night."

A Chapter of Pleasant Surprises.   125

"I am glad of that," said Mr. Dighton.

"Mind you don't tell her who has come, dear Mr. Jones," said Violet.

"Bless you, no!" he answered; "she'll soon find out, she will."

Childie did indeed wonder who her visitors

could be. She left grand-dad in Mrs. White's charge, and followed Mr. Jones down to the shop. He darted away, thinking that the two little friends would like to be alone; and Mr. Dighton had had the same thought too, for he strolled up the street, smoking a cigar.

Childie gave one little cry of surprise and delight when she saw Violet's eager face and heard her voice saying:

"Rosebud! darling Rosebud!"

She knelt down by her side, and whispered:

"Miss Violet dear, it's you," and burst into tears, resting her pale little face on Violet's lap.

It was all too much for her. But she felt Violet's loving kiss on her forehead, and she smiled through her tears.

"It's you who are the little mother now," she said; "I'm only a silly baby. But, oh, dear Miss Violet! I *am* happy you've come."

"Do you remember, Rosebud," asked Violet, "how you said that it would be a happy day when I came to see you?"

"And so it is," said Childie, her face brightening; "for grand-dad's ever so much better."

And whilst they were talking there was a heavy tread heard on the stairs, and good old Mrs. White came into the shop.

"Grand-dad is sleeping sound," she said cheerily. "Deary me, Childie, I forgot you'd a visitor."

"Don't go away," said Childie, coming from behind the counter. "My visitor would like to speak to you. I've been telling her how kind and good you've been to grand-dad and me."

Mrs. White no sooner saw who the visitor was than she put her ample arms round Violet, and called her by a string of endearing names.

"My pretty little lamb, didn't I say you'd be running faster than me one of these fine days?" she exclaimed. "My heart's-ease, my sweetheart, my little pet chicken! Deary me, to think of you coming after Rosebud and me!"

"Everything has taken a turn, hasn't it?" said Childie, smiling at Violet. "You have, and darling grand-dad has; there's no doubt about that."

"That's what the parrot says now!" cried Violet excitedly; and then she stopped suddenly

for Mr. Jones and Mr. Dighton stepped into the shop.

"There, you've been and told," said Mr. Jones, shaking his fist at her. "Oh, you naughty little lady! But you'll all come and hear for yourselves what that parrot says now. Childie, I learnt that bird to say 'Things 'ave took a turn', just as a surprise for you; and you was to have heard it the very day grand-dad fell ill. And all the time you and Mrs. White have been nursing grand-dad, that 'ere parrot has been calling this out; and I scolded awful at her, and couldn't bear to listen to her saying words which weren't true. And every time she called it, I cried 'Stop that, do you hear?' But she called it all the same; and then I threw a dark cloth over her head, and that didn't stop her prating! But now I love to hear them words; for they're all true to-day, ain't they?"

"Yes, they're all true," said Childie, smiling happily. And all her kind friends, red-nosed Mr. Jones, and dear fat Mrs. White, and fragile little Violet, and tall Mr. Dighton, were glad to see her smile again; for she had not smiled a great deal lately.

CHAPTER IX.

A NEW LEASE OF LIFE.

Every afternoon at two o'clock, the hour when Rosebud used to start for Grosvenor Square, Violet, proud in her newly-found strength, left her home for the second-hand book-shop. Sometimes Mr. Dighton wheeled her, and sometimes James. James, who had very high and mighty ideas, thought the family had all gone mad, and that he was going mad too; for he took a wonderful interest in little Rosebud's home, and once, when he was waiting in the shop, he turned over the books, and seeing one which he thought looked interesting—it was about horse-racing—he bought it then and there, and paid the money to Mr. Jones, who divided his time between birds and books, and had a great deal of exercise in running from one side of the road to the other. But he did not mind that. He would have liked to sell as many books for grand-dad as he sold canaries for himself.

"I'm selling canaries by the bushel, and linnets by the gallon," he confided to Violet. "See if I don't take one of them swell houses in Grosvenor Square before this 'ere year is gone!"

"I wish you would," said Violet, smiling at him.

"Wait a bit," he answered gravely; "don't you be in a hurry. You ain't been in a hurry to step across the road and see my place."

"Why, Mr. Jones," she replied, "you know quite well I am waiting until Rosebud feels she can leave her grandfather."

"Bless your heart, I know that," he answered. "You mustn't come without Rosebud. Why, she made us acquainted, and we shouldn't be happy without her dear little self. Ah, the many hours that 'ere child has passed with them birds in my shop! She was always for getting the seed out and feeding them. Childie ruined me in seed, specially hemp seed; and I couldn't refuse her. Who could, I wonder? 'No seed to-day, Childie,' I'd say to her, handing her a bagful against my will. Oh, she has a wonderful way about her, she has!"

That same afternoon Violet had a customer all to herself. She was sitting as usual in grand-dad's arm-chair, waiting for Childie to come down and have a cup of tea and a piece of cake, when a gentleman stepped into the shop, took a book from a certain box marked "All one shilling", and tossed the shilling on to the counter, and hurried away reading. It was only a shilling, but Violet was so proud of it that she could have eaten it!

"Who would have thought that I should sit here and sell a book for Rosebud's grandfather?" she remarked to Mr. Jones.

"Well, it is a new sort of life to you," he answered as he chinked the shilling on the counter; "and jolly nicer, too, than being shut up in that 'ere fine room of yours."

"Jolly nicer," laughed Violet, who was becoming quite merry.

And as for grand-dad himself, every morning saw him better. The doctor told Childie that he had had a very severe attack, and that at one time he did not think her grandfather would recover.

"But you never lost heart, my little dear," he said kindly.

"No, sir," she answered simply, looking up at him and smiling gravely. "When one loves, sir, it is only natural to hope, isn't it? And then you know, sir, when grand-dad has been sad and anxious about trade, I've always told him he must never lose hope; and one must practice what one preaches, mustn't one?"

"That is true enough, little girl," he replied. "At least you've done so. Well, I'm not going to tell you to take extra care of the grandfather, now that he is out of danger, for you are always thinking of his comfort, and I can trust you thoroughly. You are a famous little nurse."

"Thank you, sir," she answered, grateful for his kind words. Indeed, her heart was full of gratitude.

She sat by grand-dad's side, holding his dear hand, talking to him in her own motherly way, sometimes stitching a little, sometimes putting down her work and watching his dear face as he lay asleep, and wondering what she should have felt like if there had been no hope for his recovery. Every one of his white hairs was precious to her.

"He needed my care before he was ill," she said to herself, "but now he'll need it doubly; and, oh, won't I love him and look after him!"

Dear little heart, she had always done that. Sometimes she would look up from her work, and see his eyes fixed upon her.

"You are indeed one of God's own gracious smiles, Childie," he said once. "I am always wondering about you, and always grateful for you."

And one afternoon he asked where her dolls

were. "I miss Jane Eyre, and Robinson Crusoe, and Queen Elizabeth," he said smiling. "They were always sprawling about somewhere. I liked

to have them near me, because you were fond of them, Childie."

She took them out of a drawer, and put them tidy, and gave them a private scolding for looking so sulky and disagreeable. But that was scarcely reasonable of her; for no one would particularly enjoy being shut up in a drawer for nearly a fortnight!

"I haven't had any thoughts to spare for you," she said to Queen Elizabeth; for she felt that she owed some sort of explanation to royalty. "Grand-dad has been ill, and when those we love are ill, we can't be bothered to think about inferior people."

This was scarcely an explanation to give to a queen. It was really a lucky thing for Childie's neck that Queen Elizabeth was only a stupid powerless doll.

One day grand-dad asked Childie about the shop. "Any more books gone, dear?" he inquired.

"Several," she answered. "Trade is very good just now. Some one came yesterday and bought the fat Greek dictionary. I was very sorry to part with it. It is such an old friend, you know. The same gentleman wanted to buy the learnèd book you were reading before you were taken ill. It had your spectacles in it, grand-dad. I couldn't let it go; and your snuff-box was lying just by it on the counter. The gentleman seemed rather cross, and said I was a silly little girl."

"A very dear little girl," murmured grand-dad, smiling at her in his old proud way. He said to himself that it was indeed worth while getting well for the sake of being loved as Childie loved him.

One morning he watched her covering an old worn-out book. "Poor battered old thing," he said sympathetically. "Ah, Childie, what a glorious library that is of Mr. Dighton's! I am always thinking about it. Do you know, Childie, I've dreamt ever so many times that it belonged to me. Wasn't that a golden dream?"

"Yes, grand-dad," she answered brightly, happy to see that he was so much better. "But I wish, dear, that it was not only a dream. I wish that I had bags of money, and could buy a beautiful library like Mr. Dighton's, and give it to you. Shouldn't I be proud of myself then? I would buy every book you loved, grand-dad; and I think

I know the names of a great many of your favourite books, don't I?"

He smiled.

"Yes, Childie," he replied, "you know all about me. Why, sometimes you can tell me the number of the page where I left off, can't you?"

"Of course," she answered, "it is easy enough to learn that; and it saves you the trouble of turning over a great many pages, doesn't it? And I'm bound to put a mark in, or remember in some way or other, when I take out your spectacles and scold you for having left them in to be quashed — like poor Crusoe's arm, you know!"

He laughed quite merrily at the very thought of Childie scolding him. There was no doubt that grand-dad was now fairly on the road to recovery.

The next day he was so very much better that Childie was able to leave him, and make the long promised visit to Mr. Jones's shop, together with Violet.

Mr. Jones, who was in a high state of excitement, wanted to carry everybody across the road; but Violet said she would walk with Rosebud, and the two little friends took their first stroll together, each one's arm round the other one's waist.

"You're not frightened, dear Miss Violet?" asked the little mother.

"Of course I'm not frightened with you, Rosebud dear," answered Violet.

Mr. Jones stood at his shop door to receive his little guests.

"Ain't I just proud to see you, that's all!" he said, rubbing his hands. "Haven't I just been busy cleaning out the place nice for you? Bless your hearts, it's as spruce as any drawing-room. That's your chair, missy dear. Sit you down. And here littl'un's special stool. And make yourself at home, missy dear; for I'm blessed if I ain't particular glad to see you sitting so cosy and friendly. And that 'ere bird's the bird as we've spoken of. Only don't you just think she'll screech now that we want her to? Oh, no! Have you ever seen one of them poodles perform when people wishes them to perform? Bless you, no. They go dead sulky, they do, and won't even look cheerful."

Violet was delighted with the birds. She fell in love with a Virginian nightingale, and said she intended to buy it if Mr. Jones would part with it.

"All right, missy, one of these days," he said cheerily. "We aren't selling or buying to-day. This ain't business, this is pleasure, jolly pleasure!"

Then Childie went to a certain cupboard, and took out a certain bag, and said to Mr. Jones:

"If you please, dear Mr. Jones, may the birds have some hemp seed?"

Mr. Jones turned to Violet and laughed.

"There now, didn't I tell you as how that little child would be after the hemp seeds? Oh, she'll be the ruin of me! Who'd give me hemp seeds if I was starving, I should like to know?"

"I would," cried Violet.

"And I would," cried Childie.

"'Urrah!" said Mr. Jones, "I sha'n't come off badly then."

At that moment the parrot became rather excited. She had heard a word she recognized—the word 'urrah,—and without any hesitation she shrieked out at the top of her voice:

"Things 'ave took a turn—'urrah! things 'ave took a turn—'urrah! Say that, Donkey. Stop that, d'you hear?"

CHAPTER X.

A PLEASANT PROSPECT.

So grand-dad recovered from his illness, and came down into the old shop one afternoon, leaning on Childie's arm.

"Aren't you glad to see the dear books again?" Childie asked, as she made him comfortable in his arm-chair, and took her accustomed place by his side. "And isn't it like old times, grand-dad, for you and me and Jane Eyre and Mr. Crusoe and Queen Elizabeth to be sitting here and waiting for customers to come in? And, grand-dad darling, here is a new snuff-box for you, with beautiful fresh snuff in it. Violet has bought it for you. And see, grand-dad, I've made a new velvet skull-cap for your dear old head. Dear me! How pretty your white hair looks beneath it. I think

A Pleasant Prospect.

you are just like a picture, grand-dad; and Mrs. White thinks so too."

She had put the cap on his head, and was staring at him admiringly when Violet arrived, and was introduced to grand-dad, whom she had never seen before; and she made Rosebud feel very proud and happy by whispering:

"Oh, Rosebud darling, what a sweet old gentleman!"

Childie hugged her with delight, and said blissfully:

"Isn't he just lovely? Isn't he just beautiful?"

And then Violet had some wonderful news to give Rosebud about the country.

"Papa says you and your dear grandfather are to come with us to our country-home next week.

He is going to tell you all about it himself. Oh, you don't know how lovely it is, Rosebud. I haven't seen much of it, because I have not been able to walk about; but I love to lie on the sofa under the trees, and listen to the birds singing, and the dear cuckoo. You've never heard the cuckoo, have you?"

"No," answered Childie, her face aglow with excitement at the prospect of going to the country. "I've only heard a cuckoo-clock. Is that anything like?"

"Something," said Violet smiling; "but not like the real thing, you know. And then, Rosebud, the trees are so green, and the clouds are such a lovely shape, and the cows look so pretty in the fields. Oh, we shall be happy all together!"

"And won't the colour just come into grand-dad's cheeks!" cried Childie, laughing with glee. "Grand-dad, darling, do you hear what we are saying? Won't you just be happy reading under the trees with your poor left eye!"

"Won't the colour just come back into Childie's

cheeks," answered grand-dad, smiling at her; "pale, thin little cheeks, pale and thin because of a stupid old grandfather."

"And Mr. Jones is to come and spend his holiday with us," continued Violet breathlessly; "and of course Jane Eyre and Mr. Crusoe and Queen Elizabeth."

"Of course," said Childie gravely; "one couldn't go without them, you know. And have you told dear Mr. Jones yet?"

"No," answered Violet; "but papa will tell him."

"I think I must," said Childie eagerly. "How he will like to hear the birds singing in the trees! And how he'll love to hear the cuckoo!"

"Who'll love to hear the cuckoo?" asked Mr. Jones, popping in suddenly.

"You will," cried Childie.

"That 'ere child's mad," said Mr. Jones, staring at her. Then seeing grand-dad, he exclaimed:

"Hurrah, sir, a million welcomes to you! My word, how we've missed you down here. Them books has been quite forlorn, and we've been forlorner."

After he had chatted a little to grand-dad, he turned to Childie and said coaxingly:

"What about that 'ere cuckoo you were naming as I came?"

"I'm not going to tell you," said Childie, trying to be very haughty; but the next minute she had caught hold of his hand, and was telling him the wonderful news.

"Look here," he said, "are you poking fun at me, or is this real true?"

"It is real true!" cried the little girls delightedly, and even grand-dad joined in too.

"Well, then, I *am* took aback," he said, pulling out his handkerchief, and blowing his nose rather violently; "that's all. To think of me having a holiday; not one of them bank holidays, when it always rains cats and dogs, but a proper fine holiday with Childie, and Childie's grand-dad and little missy here. Yes, I'm took aback, I am. Why, I've not been to the country since I was a little innocent-like boy, as climbed the neighbours' trees and stole the fruit; and didn't it just taste fine! I used to hear the cuckoo then, but it's a sight of years ago."

He blew his nose again still more violently.

"You've got a cold, dear Mr. Jones," said Childie kindly.

"No, littl'un," he answered gently, "I've not got no cold; but I've got a bit of a lump in my heart with thinking about my old home in the country. And there's nothing like that, Childie, to make one just a bit sad. Begging your pardon, I think I'll just go and clean up my shop."

Childie followed him to the door, and then put up her face to be kissed.

"Dear Mr. Jones," she whispered, "I think you are an old darling, and I love you very much."

"Littl'un," he said as he lifted her up in his arms, "you've got a sweet little, sympathetic heart of your own, you have. Bless your dear, tiny, wee self."

CHAPTER XI.

GRAND-DAD'S DREAM COMES TRUE.

Before they all started for the country, Mr. Dighton and Mrs. White had a long serious consultation together in Mr. Dighton's wonderful library.

"I should not like to do anything of the kind without your advice," said Mr. Dighton; "but tell me now, Mrs. White, what do you think of my plan?"

"I think it is splendid, sir," she answered, her kind face beaming with smiles. "Deary me! I don't know what we should do without Rosebud; and Miss Violet is always her brightest when that deary child is here. And Rosebud will never leave her grand-dad now. She used to cry awful because he'd been taken ill when she wasn't with

Grand-dad's Dream Comes True. 149

him. She was always reproaching herself, and fretting her little tender heart away."

"Well, she won't do that any more," replied Mr. Dighton; "for old Mr. Burnley will be quite

happy here, looking after my library, and collecting books for me, and reading them to his soul's content. He is a scholarly old gentleman, and I shall be pleased to have him with us. Do you think Rosebud will consent to come, Mrs. White?"

"Yes, sir," replied Mrs. White; "because, begging your pardon, sir, she's awful fond of you and Miss Violet, and me too, sir, if you'll excuse me saying so. But it'll be a shocking wrench to part with her friend, Mr. Jones. That'll be the trouble, sir."

"But he shall come here just as often as he likes," said Mr. Dighton, "and he'll always be welcome. Rosebud has done so much for my little Violet that I feel I cannot do half enough for her; and Mr. Jones is my friend now as well as hers."

"I'm sure he's a very nice gentleman," said Mrs. White enthusiastically, for Mr. Jones had quite won her good-will; "and I'll be glad to do anything to make him cosy and comfortable here. You've no idea, sir, how kind that person was when Mr. Burnley was ill; and he was never tired of running errands for me, and seeing to the shop, and taking thought for me and every one. And always a cheery word on his lips. And his love for Childie is like a bit of poetry, sir."

"I see he has made a friend of you," said Mr. Dighton smiling, "so that's all right. For do they not say here that it is the best thing in the world to win Mrs. White for a friend, since she

has it all her own way at No. 12, Grosvenor Square? And a dear, good, kind way it is!"

"Thank you, sir," she said, smiling with pleasure at his words of praise.

Then Mr. Dighton, begging her not to tell Violet until he had concluded the arrangement, hurried off to the second-hand book-shop

and found Childie alone, putting the books in order and dusting them very lovingly, and looking into some of them.

"Childie," he said gently, "put these books down, and come and sit near me. I want to talk with you very seriously about grand-dad and yourself."

"Yes, sir," she answered gravely.

Then he told her that he wanted grand-dad and herself to come and live with him at Grosvenor Square, and that grand-dad would look after the library and have no troubles, and she would divide her time between him and Violet, who loved her dearly; and Mrs. White would take care of them both.

"You would be sorry to leave the old book-shop," he said kindly; "but then grand-dad is old and weary, and trade is very slack sometimes, isn't it? And grand-dad would be far happier in my library, seeing to the beautiful old manuscripts I collect, and reading my books to his heart's content, and helping me in my work."

"Oh, he *would* be happy!" she cried, as usual thinking always of him. "He would be happy!"

"And you, little Rosebud, would you be happy?" he asked anxiously.

"Oh, yes!" she answered brightly; but—"

"But what, child?" he asked, knowing quite well what she meant.

"But, dear Mr. Jones," she stammered out looking very distressed. "I love him so much, and I couldn't bear not to see him again. You see, he is my old friend; and I love my old friends better than my new ones. You are not angry with me for saying this, are you?"

"Indeed not, Rosebud," he said, taking her hand. "You have a loyal little heart, and I love you all the more for it. But you would not have to say good-bye to Mr. Jones. Why, he should come whenever he liked, and we would all be delighted to see him. You know, Childie, we look upon him as our friend too; first for your sake, and then for his own sake. He and his pipe would always be welcome, and of course you could come here to visit him as often as you liked. Does it seem so very dreadful now, Rosebud?"

"No," she answered, smiling at him through her tears. "And indeed, sir, I'm not an ungrateful little girl, for I think you are so very kind, you and dear Miss Violet and Mrs. White. I can't imagine what I've done to receive such wonderful kindness."

"Why, Childie," he said, "you have done everything for me. If it had not been for you, I believe my little girl would still be lying on the sofa day after day, finding the hours drag very wearily. But you came and made them spin away like a bicycle! And, clever little doctor that you are, you managed to put some colour into her cheeks, and some strength into her body. And so I say, 'God bless you', dear little Rosebud. And Violet loves you, and nothing would make her happier than for you and grand-dad to live with us. Do you think you could leave the old book-shop, Childie?"

"I am sure I could," she answered gently; and then she added to herself, "for grand-dad's sake."

So when grand-dad crept slowly into the shop, she left Mr. Dighton to tell him of the great plan, knowing that grand-dad would be happy beyond all words to have the charge of, and to read in, that beautiful library, which he had seen one morning before he was taken ill, and which he had spoken about so often during his illness.

But she herself ran across the road to Mr. Jones.

"Well, littl'un," he said cheerily, placing her stool for her, "and what can I serve you with this fine morning? Here's a pair of love-birds, stupid cooing things they are, to be sure, and here's a tidy little goldfinch, and a new canary as sings to knock you down; or perhaps you're thinking to buy the parrot. Buy the parrot indeed! I'll trouble you! As long as I've got a bit of a roof, that 'ere parrot will share it with me. We'll eat our last hemp seed together, she and I will."

"Of course you will," replied Childie. "Why, the parrot is part of you and you are part of the parrot! And you know, dear Mr. Jones, your nose is rather the same colour as the parrot's tail, isn't it?"

"You leave my nose alone, Childie," he said, "or else you'll leave the bird-shop. But now I look at your bit of a face, I see you've been crying a wee morsel. What's wrong, littl'un?"

"Nothing," she answered; "only I want to talk to you very, very seriously."

"Talk on," he replied; "I'm your man."

And she told him of Mr. Dighton's proposal.

"Well, now," he said, "and why aren't you looking jolly happy, and merry, and dancing about like a young kittenish thing, to think that grand-dad is going to be nicely cared for, and that 'ere old shop of yours with them shabby, stupid books is going to be sent to Jericho or some such place?"

"Oh! Mr. Jones," she cried, "I can't bear to leave you—that's what I'm fretting about."

He blew his red nose very violently.

"Look here," he said, "didn't you say as how me and my pipe were always to be welcome at that house? And me and my pipe won't stay away from that 'ere house from any shyness, I can tell you! And who's there to be frightened of in that house? Mrs. White, bless you! I wasn't ever frightened of the woman; it was her awful black bonnet concern with the violet flag waving on the top as first took me aback. When you lift the bonnet off and get to the real person, why, to be sure, it is a nice, kind person! I think a deal of Mrs. White, I do; and I know she'll take care of my Rosebud better than me or grand-dad can. So don't you be fretting for me, Childie. And there! what a happy holiday we're going to have in the country, aren't we?"

"Yes," she answered, smiling brightly.

"And then when you come back, off you go to Grosvenor Square," he continued. "Fancy me, now, having familiar-like friends in that 'ere swell part of London. Horrid, ugly place it is too, not near as snug as this shop! And hark you, Childie, these last few months things have took such a queer turn, that who knows, if I shove away my odd farthings in a seed-tin, maybe I shall come and buy one of them horrid, ugly, big houses in Grosvenor Square. So it's all settled now, Rosebud, and don't you fear that I'm going to cut you because you and grand-dad and them 'ere dolls of yours is going to be fashionable-like people! So you run across and offer Mr. Jones's respects and compliments to Mr. Dighton, and tell him as how I give my consent to the plan, and as how I'm hearty glad for grand-dad's sake and Childie's sake. Kiss me, littl'un, and then run across as hard as you can; before I change my mind, you know."

He looked after her, and rubbed his eyes.

"Well, well," he said to himself, "I'm blessed if I ever thought things would take this sort of turn. But there, now, I'm not going to growl. Grand-dad and Childie will be cosy and comfortable, and she won't have no troubles. Only it'll take a sight of them seed-tins of money before I'm able to buy one of them ugly houses in Grosvenor Square!"

CHAPTER XI.

THE OLD AND THE NEW.

Everyone at Grosvenor Square—James included—was delighted to hear the good news. I think Violet and Childie and Mrs. White must have kissed one another hundreds of times. And then Childie described to them how she told dear Mr. Jones, and how unselfish and cheerful he was. "Because, you know," she said plaintively, "he will miss me a little, won't he?"

"Of course, he will miss you ever so much," cried Violet. "But he must come and see us very often."

"The kind, good man!" exclaimed Mrs. White. "Yes, he must come and smoke his pipe and have his cup of tea whenever he likes, and I will give him such a welcome, Rosebud dear."

"I am sure you will," said Childie earnestly. "And he will come very often, I'm certain; for he has promised me, and he always keeps his word. Dear, dear Mr. Jones!"

That same evening grand-dad and Childie and Jane Eyre and Mr. Crusoe and Queen Elizabeth sat together in the old book-shop.

"It isn't any use my covering the books, grand-dad," she said, "as we are going to part with them all."

He laid his hand on her head.

"Are you sorry we are going to part with them, Childie?" he asked lovingly.

"Just a little bit, grand-dad," she answered smiling. "But then, grand-dad darling, we shall have heaps of other books to love, sha'n't we? And what I am so happy about is that you'll have no worry, no anxiety. You'll be able to read in the beautiful library just as long as you please, and when your dear old eyes are feeling tired, why, then I'll read to you. And I'll take such loving care of you, grand-dad, in our new home; for you're not strong yet, dear, no, you're not strong yet."

She had risen up, and was standing at the back

of his chair, her hands clasped around his neck, and her little head resting against his cheek.

"Dear little Childie," he murmured, there's no one like my Childie in the whole world. When I want to say how much I love her, I cannot find words half gentle enough, except when I call her one of God's brightest smiles, and one of his sweetest, fairest flowers. Books are all very well, Childie, but they are not as beautiful as flowers. And my little Rosebud, my little flower, would make any home happy for her old grand-dad."

. . . .

The weeks, the months, the years go merrily by at the great house in Grosvenor Square. Violet's strength increases together with her love for her little friend and companion, Rosebud; and Mr. Dighton blesses the day when he first went into that old second-hand book-shop, and made the acquaintance of the sweet little shopkeeper who was to become so dear to Violet and himself. Grand-dad finds pleasure and delight in working for Mr. Dighton, and collecting beautiful books and manuscripts for the splendid library, which is really the pride of his heart. And Childie loves to see him happy, and feels that she can never be thankful enough to the tall gentleman for all his kindness to grand-dad and herself.

And she is happy too, especially when a certain

red-nosed person leaves a certain bird-shop to take care of itself, and comes to have a cup of tea and a smoke with his friends in the "horrid ugly house".

He does not seem to mind it being horrid and ugly, for he comes very often, knowing full well that he will always get a hearty welcome from his own little Rosebud child, from dear old grand-dad, from little missy, from little missy's papa, from James himself, and, last not least, from kind Mrs. White.

www.ingramcontent.com/pod-product-compliance
Lightning Source LLC
Chambersburg PA
CBHW030249170426

43202CB00009B/678